JavaScr Doing

Over 100 Hands-On Coding Challenges for Mastering JS

By

Laurence Lars Svekis

Dedicated to

Alexis and Sebastian

Thank you for your support

Introduction to the Book

Welcome to "JavaScript by Doing: Over 100 Coding Challenges" the perfect guide for beginners eager to dive into the world of JavaScript. This book is structured to provide a clear, step-by-step approach to learning JavaScript by actually coding. Whether you are a complete novice or have some familiarity with programming, the exercises in this book are designed to enhance your understanding and proficiency in JavaScript. From simple variable assignments and data types to complex functions and asynchronous operations, this guide covers it all, providing both theoretical insights and practical exercises to ensure you gain a comprehensive grasp of the language.

Example Exercises for Beginners
Displaying Text: Learn to use console.log() to display messages in the browser's console.
Exercise: Write a JavaScript line of code that prints "Hello, JavaScript!" to the console.
Sample Code: console.log("Hello, JavaScript!");

Working with Variables: Introduce variable creation and manipulation.
Exercise: Declare a variable named age and set it to your age. Print this variable to the console.
Sample Code:
let age = 25; // Replace 25 with your age
console.log(age);

Basic Conditional Logic: Using simple if statements to make decisions.
Exercise: Write a program that checks if a number (e.g., 5) is even and prints a corresponding message to the console.
let number = 5;
if (number % 2 === 0) {
 console.log("The number is even.");
} else {
 console.log("The number is odd.");
}

These exercises are designed to help you start coding in JavaScript immediately, with simple yet effective tasks that build a solid foundation in programming basics. As you progress through the book, the exercises will gradually increase in complexity, preparing you for more advanced JavaScript programming challenges.

Source Code

Get the book source code at

https://github.com/lsvekis/The-JavaScript-Challenge

Learn more about JavaScript at

https://basescripts.com/

Introduction to JavaScript

What is JavaScript?
JavaScript is a programming language that allows you to implement complex features on web pages. It is the scripting language that enables you to create dynamically updating content, control multimedia, animate images, and pretty much everything else. It's what makes web pages interactive and engaging.

History of JavaScript
JavaScript was developed by Brendan Eich in 1995 and quickly became a staple of web development. Over the years, it has evolved significantly, with the ECMAScript specification standardizing the core of JavaScript, ensuring compatibility across different web browsers.

Why Learn JavaScript?
JavaScript is essential for web development. It's one of the three core technologies of the web, alongside HTML and CSS, enabling dynamic interactions on webpages. Its versatility extends beyond the browser with environments like Node.js, which allow for server-side scripting. Learning JavaScript opens doors to web and software development roles and is crucial for front-end, back-end, and full-stack development paths.

Coding Exercises Introduction

Setting Up the Environment
To run JavaScript, you typically include it within an HTML document. This setup involves creating a simple HTML file and linking a JavaScript file using a <script> tag, allowing the browser to execute the JavaScript.

Basic HTML page structure with JavaScript

```
<!DOCTYPE html>
<html>
<head>
```

```
    <title>JavaScript Practice</title>
  </head>
  <body>
    <script src="script.js"></script>
  </body>
</html>
```

Exercise: Displaying Text

The console.log() function in JavaScript is used to print any messages or variables to the browser's console. It's a helpful tool for debugging and showing output during development.

Understanding Variables

Variables in JavaScript are named containers for storing data values. JavaScript uses var, let, and const to declare variables:

- var is the oldest keyword, with function scope.
- let introduces block scope, better controlling the variable's lifetime.
- const is like let but for constants, which means the value assigned to a const variable cannot be changed.

Exercise: Working with Variables

Here's how variables are declared and used in JavaScript:

```
let message = "Hello, World!"; // Declares a variable that can be changed
const PI = 3.14159;       // Declares a constant whose value cannot be changed
var age = 30;             // Declares a variable with function scope
```

Common Data Types

JavaScript variables can store different types of values, each of which behaves differently:

- String: Represents textual data, e.g., "Alice".
- Number: An integer or a floating-point number, e.g., 25 or 3.14.
- Boolean: Represents a logical entity and can have two values: true or false.
- Null: An assignment value that represents no value or a null value.

- Undefined: A variable that has been declared but not assigned a value is automatically assigned the value undefined.
- Object: Collections of properties, can be seen as a collection of key-value pairs. Arrays in JavaScript are a type of object.
- Array: A global object that is used in the construction of arrays; a high-level list-like object.

Exercise: Exploring Data Types
Here's how to demonstrate different data types in JavaScript:

```javascript
let name = "Alice";
let age = 25;
let isStudent = true;
let address = null;
let definition;
console.log(typeof name);       // Outputs "string"
console.log(typeof age);        // Outputs "number"
console.log(typeof isStudent);  // Outputs "boolean"
console.log(typeof address);    // Outputs "object" because
`null` is treated as an object
console.log(typeof definition); // Outputs "undefined"
```

Basic Conditional Logic

Introduction to if Statements
The if statement is used to execute a statement or block of code if a specified condition is true. It can be paired with else and else if to handle multiple conditions and provide alternate execution paths.

Exercise: Using Conditional Logic
Here's an example showing how to use conditional logic based on the value of a variable:
```javascript
let score = 85;
if (score >= 90) {
 console.log("Excellent");
} else if (score >= 80) {
 console.log("Good");
} else {
```

```
  console.log("Needs Improvement");
}
```

Combining Strings

Concatenating strings can be done using the + operator or template literals (backticks), which allow for embedded expressions.

Exercise: Create a Greeting

Here's how you can use both methods to concatenate strings:
```
let user = "Alice";
let greeting = "Hello, " + user + "! Welcome to JavaScript."; // Using the + operator
console.log(greeting);
console.log(`Hello, ${user}! Welcome to JavaScript.`); // Using template literals
```

Coding Exercises

Hello, JavaScript!

Task: Write a JavaScript program that prints "Hello, JavaScript!" to the console.

Purpose: Familiarize with basic output in JavaScript.

Sample Code:
```
console.log("Hello, JavaScript!");
```

Explanation:

This exercise introduces you to the console.log() method, which is used to print any message you want to the console. Here, the message "Hello, JavaScript!" is displayed in the console, demonstrating the simplest way to output information in JavaScript.

Variable Assignments

Task: Declare two variables, a and b. Assign 5 to a and 6 to b. Then create a third variable c that holds the sum of a and b. Print c to the console.

Purpose: Practice declaring variables and performing arithmetic operations.

Sample Code:

```
let a = 5;
let b = 6;
let c = a + b;
console.log(c);
```

Explanation:

This exercise introduces variable declarations using let, which is a keyword used to declare variables that can have block scope and be reassigned. Here, a and b are assigned numerical values, which are then added together and assigned to c. Finally, c is printed to the console, showing the result of the arithmetic operation.

Data Type Exploration

Task: Create variables of different data types: number, string, boolean, null, and undefined. Use the typeof operator to print the type of each variable to the console.

Purpose: Understand different data types and the typeof operator.

Sample Code:

```
let number = 42;
let string = "JavaScript";
let boolean = true;
let nothing = null;
let undefinedVariable;
console.log(typeof number); // "number"
console.log(typeof string); // "string"
console.log(typeof boolean); // "boolean"
```

```
console.log(typeof nothing); // "object" (quirk in JavaScript)
console.log(typeof undefinedVariable); // "undefined"
```
Explanation:
This exercise explores different data types in JavaScript. typeof is an operator used to determine the type of a variable. This is useful for debugging or to ensure variables are of expected types before they are manipulated in functions or conditions.

Basic Conditional Logic

Task: Write a JavaScript program that uses a conditional statement to check if a number stored in a variable is even. If it is, print "The number is even" to the console.
Purpose: Apply conditional statements and understand modulus operator usage.
Sample Code:
```
let number = 24;
if (number % 2 === 0) {
 console.log("The number is even");
}
```
Explanation:
This exercise introduces the use of conditional (if) statements and the modulus operator (%). The modulus operator returns the remainder of a division operation. In this case, it checks whether a number is even by dividing it by 2 and checking if the remainder is 0.

String Concatenation

Task: Declare two string variables, concatenate them, and print the result. Example variables could be firstName and lastName.
Purpose: Learn string manipulation and concatenation.
Sample Code:
```
let firstName = "John";
let lastName = "Doe";
let fullName = firstName + " " + lastName;
```

console.log(fullName);

Explanation:

This exercise demonstrates how to concatenate strings using the + operator. Two string variables firstName and lastName are created and concatenated with a space between them to form a full name. The resulting string is then printed to the console, illustrating basic string manipulation.

These exercises cover fundamental concepts and provide a hands-on way to learn JavaScript syntax and operations.

Control Structures and Data Handling

Control Structures and Data Handling
Control structures are fundamental programming constructs that allow you to control the flow of execution based on conditions or repeatedly execute a block of code. Data handling involves operations on data like creating, retrieving, manipulating, and storing data within your program.
Control Structures Include:

- Conditional statements (if, else, switch)
- Loops (for, while, do-while)

Data Handling:

- Manipulating strings, arrays, and objects.
- Checking data types and converting between them.

Simple Conditionals
Conditionals are used to execute different code branches based on conditions. The simplest form is the if statement.
Example: Simple if Statement
Let's say we want to print out whether a user is an adult based on their age:

```
let age = 20;
if (age >= 18) {
  console.log("You are an adult.");
} else {
  console.log("You are not an adult.");
}
```

In this example, the code checks if age is greater than or equal to 18. If true, it prints "You are an adult"; otherwise, it prints "You are not an adult."

Loop Through Numbers
Loops are used to execute a block of code repeatedly under controlled conditions. A for loop is particularly useful for iterating over a sequence of numbers.
Example: Using a for Loop to Iterate Numbers
Suppose we want to print numbers from 1 to 10:

```
for (let i = 1; i <= 10; i++) {
```

```
console.log(i);
}
```

This for loop starts with i = 1 and runs as long as i is less than or equal to 10. After each iteration, i is incremented by 1, and the current value of i is printed.

Data Type Checking
JavaScript is a dynamically typed language, which means variables are not directly associated with any particular type, and any variable can be assigned and re-assigned values of all types.
Example: Checking Data Types
To ensure proper handling of variables, you might need to check their data types using the typeof operator.

```
let name = "Alice";
let age = 25;
let isStudent = false;
console.log(typeof name); // Outputs "string"
console.log(typeof age); // Outputs "number"
console.log(typeof isStudent); // Outputs "boolean"
```

In this example, typeof is used to determine and print the type of various variables. This is especially useful in functions where you need to validate inputs or in scripts where the data type can affect the execution logic.

Coding Exercises

Here's a detailed set of coding exercises and multiple-choice quiz questions focused on "Control Structures and Data Handling" in JavaScript, designed to enhance understanding through practical coding and theoretical questioning.

Simple Conditionals

Task: Write a JavaScript program that checks if a number is positive, negative, or zero. Use if-else conditions.

Purpose: Understand how to use conditional statements to handle multiple conditions.

Sample Code:

```
let number = -3;
if (number > 0) {
 console.log("The number is positive.");
} else if (number < 0) {
 console.log("The number is negative.");
} else {
 console.log("The number is zero.");
}
```

Explanation:

This code snippet uses if, else if, and else to check three conditions: if number is greater than 0, it's positive; if less than 0, it's negative; otherwise, it's zero. This exercise teaches the basic structure and application of conditional statements in JavaScript.

Loop Through Numbers

Task: Use a for loop to print numbers from 1 to 10.

Purpose: Learn to use loops to execute repetitive tasks.

Sample Code:

```
for (let i = 1; i <= 10; i++) {
 console.log(i);
}
```

Explanation:

This example demonstrates the use of a for loop, where i is initialized at 1 and increments by 1 on each iteration until it reaches 10. This helps in understanding loop setup and iteration.

Array Iteration

Task: Create an array of five fruits and use a for loop to print each fruit to the console.

Purpose: Practice array creation and iteration using loops.

Sample Code:

```
let fruits = ["apple", "banana", "cherry", "date", "elderberry"];
for (let i = 0; i < fruits.length; i++) {
 console.log(fruits[i]);
}
```

Explanation:

This exercise uses an array containing strings and a loop that iterates based on the array's length, accessing each element by its index and printing it. It illustrates how to manipulate arrays and loop through them.

Using Switch Cases

Task: Write a program using a switch case to print the name of the day based on a given number (1-7).

Purpose: Understand the use of switch-case statements for multi-branch selection.

Sample Code:

```
let dayNumber = 3; // Example number
switch (dayNumber) {
 case 1:
 console.log("Sunday");
 break;
 case 2:
 console.log("Monday");
 break;
 case 3:
 console.log("Tuesday");
 break;
 case 4:
 console.log("Wednesday");
 break;
 case 5:
 console.log("Thursday");
 break;
 case 6:
 console.log("Friday");
 break;
 case 7:
```

```
console.log("Saturday");
break;
default:
console.log("Invalid day number");
}
```

Explanation:
The switch-case structure allows handling multiple possible values for a variable efficiently. Each case represents a possible value of dayNumber, with a corresponding action to print the day's name.

Data Type Checking

Task: Create variables of different data types and use an if-else chain to check and print the type of each variable.
Purpose: Learn to identify and handle different data types in conditional logic.
Sample Code:

```
let items = [42, "hello", true, null, undefined];
items.forEach(item => {
if (typeof item === "number") {
console.log(`${item} is a number`);
} else if (typeof item === "string") {
console.log(`${item} is a string`);
} else if (typeof item === "boolean") {
console.log(`${item} is a boolean`);
} else if (item === null) {
console.log(`null value`);
} else {
console.log(`undefined value`);
}
});
```

Explanation:

This code iterates through an array with various data types and checks each type using typeof and strict comparison. This exercise helps in understanding how to handle different types of data in JavaScript.

Multiple Choice Quiz Questions

What will the following loop print?
```
for (let i = 0; i < 5; i++) {
 console.log(i);
}
```
A) 0, 1, 2, 3, 4
B) 1, 2, 3, 4, 5
C) 0, 1, 2, 3, 4, 5
D) 1, 2, 3, 4
Correct Answer: A) 0, 1, 2, 3, 4
Explanation: The loop starts at 0 and increments until it is less than 5, thus printing 0 to 4.

Which data type is not directly supported by JavaScript?
A) int
B) string
C) boolean
D) object
Correct Answer: A) int
Explanation: JavaScript does not have an int type; it has number to represent both integers and floating-point numbers.

What will the following code output if the input is 8?
```
let input = 8;
switch (input % 2) {
 case 0:
 console.log("Even");
 break;
 case 1:
```

```
console.log("Odd");
break;
}
```
A) Even
B) Odd
C) Error
D) None of the above
Correct Answer: A) Even
Explanation: input % 2 yields 0 for even numbers, which matches the first case in the switch statement.

Which operator is used to concatenate strings in JavaScript?
A) +
B) &
C) concat
D) append
Correct Answer: A) +
Explanation: The + operator is used to concatenate strings, combining them into one.

What is the purpose of the break statement in a switch-case?
A) To stop the case condition from being true
B) To exit the loop
C) To prevent the case from falling through to the next one
D) To break out of the program
Correct Answer: C) To prevent the case from falling through to the next one
Explanation: In a switch-case, break is used to exit the switch block, stopping subsequent cases from executing once a match is found.

These exercises and questions offer practical and theoretical insights into JavaScript's control structures and data handling, providing a robust foundation for more advanced programming concepts.

Conditional Statements

JavaScript supports several types of conditional statements:
- if statement: Executes a block of code if the specified condition is true.
- else statement: Executes a block of code if the condition in the if statement is false.
- else if statement: Specifies a new condition to test, if the first condition is false.
- switch statement: Specifies many alternative blocks of code to be executed.

If-Else Statement

The if-else statement is the fundamental control structure that allows JavaScript to make decisions. The syntax is:

```
if (condition) {
// Code to execute if the condition is true
} else {
// Code to execute if the condition is false
}
```

condition: This can be any expression that evaluates to true or false. If the condition is true, the code inside the if block runs; otherwise, the code inside the else block runs.

Else-If Ladder

When you have multiple conditions to evaluate, you can use an "else if" ladder, which is a series of if statements that are checked in sequence.

```
if (condition1) {
// Code runs if condition1 is true
} else if (condition2) {
// Code runs if condition1 is false and condition2 is true
} else {
// Code runs if all preceding conditions are false
}
```

condition1, condition2, etc.: These are evaluated in order until one is found to be true. Once a true condition is found, its associated block of code runs, and the rest of the conditions are not evaluated.

Modulus Operator (%)

The modulus operator returns the remainder of a division of two numbers. It is frequently used to check if a number is even or odd:

```
if (number % 2 === 0) {
 console.log("The number is even.");
} else {
 console.log("The number is odd.");
}
```

number % 2: This operation checks the remainder when number is divided by 2. An even number has no remainder (0), while an odd number has a remainder of 1.

Logical Operators

Logical operators such as && (logical AND) and || (logical OR) are used to combine multiple conditions.

```
if ((year % 4 === 0 && year % 100 !== 0) || (year % 400
=== 0)) {
 console.log(year + " is a leap year.");
}
```

- && and ||: In the leap year check:
- year % 4 === 0 && year % 100 !== 0: The year must be divisible by 4 and not divisible by 100.
- year % 400 === 0: Alternatively, the year can be divisible by 400.
- The || operator means that if either set of conditions is true, the year is a leap year.

Lowercase Conversion for String Comparison

To ensure that user input is compared in a case-insensitive manner, strings are often converted to a consistent case (lower or upper) before comparison.

```
if (input.toLowerCase() === "hello") {
 console.log("Hello! Nice to meet you.");
}
```

toLowerCase(): This method converts a string to all lower case, facilitating case-insensitive comparisons, which makes the program more robust and user-friendly.

These elements collectively form the backbone of many simple yet essential JavaScript programs. Understanding these basics paves the way for writing more complex and functional scripts.

Coding Exercises on Conditional Statements

Conditional Statements if, else, and switch for making decisions in code. Here is a comprehensive set of coding exercises and multiple-choice quiz questions focused on learning conditional statements in JavaScript, including if, else, and switch. These exercises and questions are designed to help understand decision-making processes in coding through practical application and assessment.

Check Age for Voting Eligibility

Task: Write a JavaScript program that determines if a person is eligible to vote based on their age. Assume voting age is 18.
Purpose: Practice using if-else statements to make decisions.
Sample Code:

```
let age = 20;
if (age >= 18) {
 console.log("You are eligible to vote.");
} else {
 console.log("You are not eligible to vote yet.");
}
```

Explanation:
This exercise uses an if-else statement to check whether the age variable meets the minimum voting age requirement. If true, it prints a message indicating eligibility; otherwise, it indicates ineligibility.

Grade Classification

Task: Classify a student's grade based on a numerical score: A (90 and above), B (80-89), C (70-79), D (60-69), F (below 60).
Purpose: Learn to handle multiple conditions in a sequence.
Sample Code:

```
let score = 85;
if (score >= 90) {
 console.log("A");
} else if (score >= 80) {
 console.log("B");
} else if (score >= 70) {
 console.log("C");
} else if (score >= 60) {
 console.log("D");
} else {
 console.log("F");
}
```

Explanation:
The if-else if structure provides a clear path for checking multiple overlapping conditions. This program uses this structure to classify scores into letter grades.

Response Based on User Input

Task: Write a JavaScript program that prompts the user for a type of weather (sunny, rainy, snowy) and gives a corresponding activity recommendation.
Purpose: Utilize switch statement to execute different blocks of code based on user input.
Sample Code:

```
let weather = prompt("Enter the weather (sunny, rainy,
snowy):");
switch (weather.toLowerCase()) {
 case "sunny":
 console.log("Let's go for a walk!");
```

```
break;
case "rainy":
console.log("Bring an umbrella!");
break;
case "snowy":
console.log("Time to build a snowman!");
break;
default:
console.log("That's not a valid weather type!");
}
```

Explanation:

This code demonstrates how to use a switch statement to handle multiple possible strings as input. It processes different activities based on weather conditions.

Even or Odd Number

Task: Write a program that checks if a number is even or odd and prints an appropriate message.

Purpose: Apply modulus operator with conditional logic to determine number properties.

Sample Code:

```
let number = 7;
if (number % 2 === 0) {
 console.log("The number is even.");
} else {
 console.log("The number is odd.");
}
```

Explanation:

The modulus operator % is used to find the remainder of the division of number by 2. If the remainder is 0, the number is even; otherwise, it's odd.

Leap Year Checker

Task: Determine whether a given year is a leap year.
Purpose: Use nested conditional statements to check for
multiple criteria in a decision-making process.
Sample Code:

```
let year = 2024;
if (year % 4 === 0) {
 if (year % 100 === 0) {
 if (year % 400 === 0) {
 console.log(`${year} is a leap year.`);
 } else {
 console.log(`${year} is not a leap year.`);
 }
 } else {
 console.log(`${year} is a leap year.`);
 }
} else {
 console.log(`${year} is not a leap year.`);
}
```

Explanation:
This exercise involves checking a year for leap year status using
nested if statements. A year is a leap year if it is divisible by 4,
but years divisible by 100 are not leap years unless they are also
divisible by 400.

Multiple Choice Quiz Questions

What will the following code output if x = 9?

```
if (x % 3 === 0) {
 console.log("Fizz");
} else {
 console.log("Buzz");
}
```

A) Fizz

B) Buzz

C) FizzBuzz

D) Nothing

Correct Answer: A) Fizz

Explanation: Since 9 is divisible by 3, the condition x % 3 === 0 is true, thus it prints "Fizz".

What is the purpose of the default case in a switch statement?

A) To specify the ending of the switch

B) To handle any case that is not explicitly handled by the switch cases

C) To break out of the switch block

D) To declare default variables

Correct Answer: B) To handle any case that is not explicitly handled by the switch cases

Explanation: The default case in a switch statement is used to execute a block of code when none of the other case conditions match the switch expression.

Which statement about the else clause in JavaScript is true?

A) It must always follow an if statement.

B) It can stand alone without an if statement.

C) It executes a block of code if the preceding if statement is true.

D) It requires its own condition.

Correct Answer: A) It must always follow an if statement.

Explanation: The else clause is used to execute a block of code when the condition in the preceding if statement is false. It cannot stand alone without an if.

What will the following code print?

```
let fruit = "apple";
switch (fruit) {
 case "banana":
```

```
console.log("Yellow");
break;
case "apple":
console.log("Red");
break;
default:
console.log("Unknown");
}
```
A) Yellow
B) Red
C) Unknown
D) Nothing
Correct Answer: B) Red
Explanation: Since the variable fruit matches the case "apple", it executes the associated block and prints "Red".

Which operator is commonly used to check equality and type in a condition?
A) ==
B) =
C) ===
D) !=
Correct Answer: C) ===
Explanation: The === operator checks both the value and the type of the variables, which is recommended for more accurate and predictable results in conditions.

These exercises and questions provide a structured approach to mastering conditional statements in JavaScript, enhancing logical thinking and coding precision in various scenarios.

Loops

Let's explore the concepts of loops in JavaScript, including their syntax and usage. Loops are fundamental for automating repetitive tasks by executing a block of code multiple times under certain conditions. I'll cover the different types of loops used in JavaScript, namely for, while, do...while, and provide explanations of their syntax and common uses, including handling nested loops and breaking out of loops.

for Loop
The for loop is one of the most common loops in JavaScript. It is used when the number of iterations is known before the loop starts. The syntax of a for loop is:

```
for (initialization; condition; increment) {
  // Code to execute on each iteration
}
```

- Initialization: Typically used to initialize a counter variable.
- Condition: The loop continues to execute as long as this condition is true.
- Increment: Updates the loop counter each time the loop is executed.

Example: Counting with a for Loop

```
for (let i = 1; i <= 10; i++) {
  console.log(i); // This will print numbers from 1 to 10
}
```

In this example, i starts at 1 and increments by 1 each loop iteration until it exceeds 10, at which point the loop stops.

while Loop
A while loop continues to run as long as its condition is true. It's useful when the number of iterations is not known beforehand.

```
while (condition) {
  // Code to execute as long as condition is true
}
```

Example: While Loop Basics

```
let i = 1;
```

```
while (i <= 10) {
 console.log(i);
 i++;
}
```

Here, the loop will execute as long as i is less than or equal to 10. It's crucial to increment i inside the loop to avoid an infinite loop.

do...while Loop

The do...while loop is similar to the while loop, but it guarantees that the body of the loop will run at least once because the condition is checked after the loop's body.

```
do {
 // Code to execute
} while (condition);
```

Example: Do...While Loop Example

```
let i = 1;
do {
 console.log(i);
 i++;
} while (i <= 10);
```

This loop will print numbers from 1 to 10. Unlike the while loop, the do...while loop's condition is evaluated after the first iteration.

Nested for Loops

Nested loops are loops inside another loop. They are commonly used for iterating over multi-dimensional data structures.

```
for (let i = 0; i < n; i++) {
 for (let j = 0; j < m; j++) {
 // Code to execute
 }
}
```

Example: Nested for Loops

```
for (let i = 0; i < 3; i++) {
 for (let j = 0; j < 3; j++) {
 console.log(`Row ${i}, Column ${j}`);
 }
```

```
}
```

This will output a grid position for each element in a 3x3 matrix.

Breaking Out of a Loop
The break statement is used to immediately exit a loop, regardless of the loop's condition.
```
for (let i = 1; i <= 10; i++) {
if (i === 6) {
break; // Exits the loop when i is 6
}
console.log(i);
}
```

In this scenario, the loop will print numbers from 1 to 5. When i equals 6, the break statement is executed, which stops the loop.

Understanding these loop constructs is crucial for writing efficient JavaScript code that needs to handle repetitive tasks or iterate over data structures. Each type of loop offers different benefits depending on the situation, providing flexibility in how code execution is handled.

Coding Exercises on JavaScript Loops

Loops: for, while, and do...while loops for repeating actions. Here's a detailed set of coding exercises and multiple-choice quiz questions focused on understanding and using different types of loops in JavaScript: for, while, and do...while. These exercises and questions are designed to help learners grasp the concept of loops for automating repetitive tasks in programming.

Counting with a for Loop

Task: Use a for loop to print numbers from 1 to 10.
Purpose: Familiarize with the syntax and usage of for loops.

Sample Code:
```
for (let i = 1; i <= 10; i++) {
 console.log(i);
}
```
Explanation:
This simple for loop starts with i initialized at 1. The loop runs as long as i is less than or equal to 10. With each iteration, i is incremented by 1 (i++), and its value is printed to the console.

While Loop Basics

Task: Use a while loop to print numbers from 10 down to 1.
Purpose: Understand how to use while loops for decremental sequences.
Sample Code:
```
let i = 10;
while (i > 0) {
 console.log(i);
 i--;
}
```
Explanation:
This while loop starts with i at 10 and continues to run as long as i is greater than 0. Inside the loop, i's value is printed before it is decremented by 1 (i--). This loop demonstrates controlling the loop with decrementing values.

Do...While Loop Example

Task: Use a do...while loop to repeatedly ask the user for a number until they enter 0.
Purpose: Learn how do...while loops ensure the loop body executes at least once.
Sample Code:
```
let number;
do {
```

```
number = parseInt(prompt("Enter a number (0 to stop):"),
10);
console.log("You entered:", number);
} while (number !== 0);
```
Explanation:
The do...while loop differs from the while loop because it
executes its body at least once before checking the condition.
In this case, it prompts the user for a number and prints it,
continuing until the user enters 0.

Nested for Loops

Task: Use nested for loops to print a 5x5 grid of asterisks (*).
Purpose: Practice using nested loops for generating multi-
dimensional structures.
Sample Code:
```
for (let i = 0; i < 5; i++) {
let line = '';
  for (let j = 0; j < 5; j++) {
line += '* ';
  }
  console.log(line);
}
```
Explanation:
This exercise uses two nested for loops. The outer loop iterates
five times (once for each row), and the inner loop iterates five
times for each outer loop iteration (once for each column),
creating a line of asterisks which is printed before the next line
starts.

Breaking Out of a Loop

Task: Write a for loop that prints numbers from 1 to 100, but
stops when it reaches a number that is divisible by 10.

Purpose: Learn how to use the break statement to exit a loop early.

Sample Code:

```
for (let i = 1; i <= 100; i++) {
if (i % 10 === 0) {
console.log("Breaking at:", i);
break;
}
console.log(i);
}
```

Explanation:

This for loop checks each number from 1 to 100 to see if it is divisible by 10 using the modulus operator (%). When it finds the first number that meets this condition, it prints that number, executes a break statement to exit the loop, and stops further iterations.

Multiple Choice Quiz Questions

What is the output of the following while loop?

```
let num = 5;
while (num > 8) {
console.log(num);
num--;
}
```

A) 5
B) Nothing
C) 8
D) Error

Correct Answer: B) Nothing

Explanation: Since the condition num > 8 is false initially (5 is not greater than 8), the loop body does not execute, and nothing is printed.

Which statement about do...while loops is true?

A) The condition is checked before the first execution of the loop body.

B) It is identical to the while loop in every aspect.

C) The loop body is executed at least once regardless of the condition.

D) The loop cannot use break or continue statements.

Correct Answer: C) The loop body is executed at least once regardless of the condition

Explanation: A do...while loop guarantees that the loop body will execute at least once, even if the condition is initially false, because the condition check occurs after the loop body's execution.

What will the following nested loops print?

```
for (let i = 0; i < 2; i++) {
for (let j = 0; j < 3; j++) {
console.log(i, j);
}
}
```

A) 0 0, 0 1, 0 2, 1 0, 1 1, 1 2

B) 0 1, 0 2, 0 3, 1 1, 1 2, 1 3

C) 0 0, 0 1, 1 0, 1 1

D) 0 0, 1 0, 2 0, 0 1, 1 1, 2 1

Correct Answer: A) 0 0, 0 1, 0 2, 1 0, 1 1, 1 2

Explanation: The outer loop iterates twice (for i values of 0 and 1), and for each iteration of the outer loop, the inner loop iterates three times (for j values of 0, 1, and 2), resulting in six print statements.

How can you immediately exit a loop in JavaScript?

A) exit()

B) break

C) continue

D) return

Correct Answer: B) break

Explanation: The break statement is used to exit a loop immediately, skipping any remaining iterations and moving control out of the loop body.

Which loop is most suitable when the number of iterations is not known beforehand?
A) for loop
B) while loop
C) do...while loop
D) Both B and C
Correct Answer: D) Both B and C
Explanation: Both while and do...while loops are suitable when the number of iterations is not predetermined, as they continue to loop based on a condition, rather than a counter.

These exercises and quiz questions provide a thorough introduction to using loops in JavaScript, helping learners practice essential programming skills for automating and simplifying repetitive tasks.

Functions

Let's delve into the concept of functions in JavaScript, a crucial part of writing maintainable, reusable code. Functions allow you to encapsulate code that performs a specific task and call it from various points in your program. Here, I'll explain the syntax and different aspects of functions, including basic definitions, parameter handling, variable scope, and function expressions.

Basic Function Definition and Invocation

A function is defined using the function keyword, followed by a name, a set of parentheses () which can optionally contain parameters, and a block of code enclosed in curly braces {}.

```
function greet() {
 console.log("Hello, world!");
}
```

Invocation: To run the function, you use the function name followed by parentheses.

```
greet(); // Calls the function, outputting "Hello, world!"
```

Function with Parameters

Functions can be designed to accept parameters, which are variables used to pass values into functions.

```
function greet(name) {
 console.log("Hello, " + name + "!");
}
```

Invocation with Parameters:

```
greet("Alice"); // Outputs: "Hello, Alice!"
```

In this example, name is a parameter that the function greet uses to customize the greeting.

Default Parameters

Default parameters allow you to initialize functions with default values. A default parameter kicks in when the argument is not provided or is undefined.

```
function greet(name = "Guest") {
 console.log("Hello, " + name + "!");
}
```

Using Default Parameters:

```
greet("Alice"); // Outputs: "Hello, Alice!"
```

greet(); // Outputs: "Hello, Guest!" because no argument is provided

Scope of Variables Inside Functions

Variables declared inside a function cannot be accessed from outside the function. This is known as the function scope. Variables within a function are local to the function.

```
function sum() {
 let a = 5; // Local variable
 let b = 3; // Local variable
 console.log(a + b); // Works fine, outputs 8
}
sum();
console.log(a); // Error: a is not defined
```

In this example, a and b are only accessible within the sum function.

Function Expression

A function expression involves defining a function inside an expression. You can assign a function to a variable. Function expressions can be anonymous; they do not need to have a name.

```
const greet = function(name) {
 console.log("Hello, " + name + "!");
};
```

Calling a Function Expression:

```
greet("Alice"); // Outputs: "Hello, Alice!"
```

Function expressions are useful because they allow you to create functions at runtime, assign them to variables, and pass them around as arguments to other functions.

Each of these function types and behaviors allows JavaScript developers to create flexible, modular, and reusable code. Understanding when and how to use each type can significantly enhance your ability to write effective JavaScript code.

Coding Exercises on JavaScript Functions

Functions: Definition, invocation, parameters, return values, and scope. Here's a detailed set of coding exercises and multiple-choice quiz questions focusing on JavaScript functions, including their definition, invocation, parameters, return values, and scope.

Basic Function Definition and Invocation

Task: Write a JavaScript function named greet that prints "Hello, World!" to the console.
Purpose: Learn how to define and call a simple function.
Sample Code:
```
function greet() {
 console.log("Hello, World!");
}
greet(); // Function invocation
```
Explanation:
This exercise demonstrates the basic structure of a function in JavaScript. The greet function is defined using the function keyword followed by the name of the function. It encapsulates a console log statement and is called (invoked) by its name followed by parentheses.

Function with Parameters

Task: Define a function named add that takes two parameters and returns their sum.
Purpose: Practice writing functions that take parameters and understand how to return a value.
Sample Code:
```
function add(a, b) {
 return a + b;
}
console.log(add(5, 3)); // Outputs 8
```
41

Explanation:
The add function demonstrates functions with parameters and a return statement. It receives two arguments, a and b, adds them, and returns the sum. The return statement sends this value back to where the function was called.

Default Parameters

Task: Create a function named multiply that multiplies two numbers. Assign a default value of 1 to both parameters.
Purpose: Understand default parameter values in functions.
Sample Code:

```
function multiply(a = 1, b = 1) {
  return a * b;
}
console.log(multiply(4)); // Outputs 4
console.log(multiply(4, 5)); // Outputs 20
```

Explanation:
This function utilizes default parameters. If the function is called with less than two arguments, the missing arguments are assigned a default value of 1. This prevents errors and allows the function to operate with fewer inputs.

Scope of Variables Inside Functions

Task: Demonstrate the scope of a variable by defining a variable inside a function and trying to access it outside the function.
Purpose: Explore the concept of local scope within functions.
Sample Code:

```
function showNumber() {
  let num = 10; // Local variable
  console.log(num); // Accessible here
}
showNumber();
```

```
console.log(num); // Error: num is not defined
```
Explanation:
The variable num is defined inside the showNumber function, making it local to that function. It cannot be accessed outside the function, illustrating the concept of local scope.

Function Expression

Task: Write a function expression that calculates the square of a number and use it immediately after.
Purpose: Understand function expressions and how they differ from function declarations.
Sample Code:
```
const square = function(num) {
 return num * num;
};
console.log(square(4)); // Outputs 16
```
Explanation:
This exercise shows a function expression where the function is assigned to the variable square. Unlike function declarations, function expressions are not hoisted, meaning they cannot be called before they are defined in the code.

Multiple Choice Quiz Questions

What will happen if you try to call a function before it is defined in JavaScript?
A) It will throw an error.
B) It will return undefined.
C) It will work if it's a function declaration.
D) It will work only if it's a function expression.
Correct Answer: C) It will work if it's a function declaration

Explanation: Function declarations are hoisted in JavaScript, which means they are moved to the top of their containing scope during the compile phase, allowing them to be called before they are defined.

What is a correct example of a function with default parameters?
A) function multiply(a, b = 1) { return a * b; }
B) function multiply(a = 1, b) { return a * b; }
C) function multiply(a, b) { return a * b = 1; }
D) function multiply(a = 1, b) { return a * b = 1; }
Correct Answer: A) function multiply(a, b = 1) { return a * b; }
Explanation: This is the correct way to set default parameters in JavaScript functions. The second parameter b is given a default value of 1.

What does the following function return?
function checkNum(num) {
if (num > 10) {
return true;
}
}
console.log(checkNum(8));
A) true
B) false
C) undefined
D) 0
Correct Answer: C) undefined
Explanation: Since the condition num > 10 is not met and there is no else part, the function returns undefined for any input less than or equal to 10.

Which statement about the scope of variables in JavaScript is true?
A) Variables defined inside a function are accessible globally.

B) Variables defined with var inside a function are local to the function.

C) Variables defined with let inside a function can be accessed anywhere in the script.

D) Global variables can only be accessed inside functions.

Correct Answer: B) Variables defined with var inside a function are local to the function

Explanation: Variables declared with var inside a function have local scope to that function, meaning they can only be accessed within that function.

Which is an example of a function expression in JavaScript?

A) function add(a, b) { return a + b; }

B) const subtract = function(a, b) { return a - b; };

C) subtract(a, b) { return a - b; }

D) function multiply(a, b);

Correct Answer: B) const subtract = function(a, b) { return a - b; };

Explanation: A function expression involves defining a function and assigning it to a variable, as shown in option B. Unlike function declarations, function expressions are not hoisted.

These exercises and quiz questions comprehensively cover the key aspects of functions in JavaScript, enhancing both practical coding skills and theoretical understanding.

Arrays and Objects

Let's explore the concepts of arrays and objects in JavaScript, which are fundamental data structures for organizing and storing data efficiently. I'll explain how to create, access, modify, and iterate over arrays and objects, using straightforward examples.

Creating and Accessing an Array

Arrays in JavaScript are used to store multiple values in a single variable. They are ordered, and each item can be accessed by its index.

Creating an Array:

let fruits = ["Apple", "Banana", "Cherry"];

Accessing Elements:

console.log(fruits[0]); // Outputs: "Apple"

console.log(fruits[1]); // Outputs: "Banana"

In this example, fruits is an array that stores three strings. Each element is accessed using its index, which starts at 0.

Adding and Removing Elements in an Array

JavaScript arrays are dynamic, meaning you can add or remove items at any time using various methods.

Adding Elements:

fruits.push("Orange"); // Adds "Orange" to the end of the array

fruits.unshift("Mango"); // Adds "Mango" to the beginning of the array

Removing Elements:

fruits.pop(); // Removes the last item ("Orange") from the array

fruits.shift(); // Removes the first item ("Mango") from the array

push and pop manipulate the end of the array, while unshift and shift affect the beginning of the array.

Creating and Accessing an Object

Objects in JavaScript are collections of properties, where each property is a key-value pair. Properties can be accessed using dot notation or bracket notation.

Creating an Object:

```
let person = {
 name: "Alice",
 age: 25,
 isStudent: true
};
```

Accessing Properties:

```
console.log(person.name); // Outputs: "Alice"
console.log(person['age']); // Outputs: 25
```

Here, person is an object with three properties: name, age, and isStudent. You can access the properties using either dot notation or bracket notation.

Updating Object Properties

You can easily modify the properties of an object after its creation.

Updating Properties:

```
person.age = 26; // Changes the age from 25 to 26
person['isStudent'] = false; // Changes isStudent from true to false
```

This modifies the age and isStudent properties of the person object.

Iterating Over an Array of Objects

When you have an array of objects, you may need to iterate over it to access or modify each object. JavaScript provides several ways to do this, such as using for loops or array methods like forEach.

Array of Objects:

```
let people = [
 { name: "Alice", age: 25 },
 { name: "Bob", age: 30 },
 { name: "Carol", age: 22 }
];
```

Iterating Over the Array:

```javascript
people.forEach(function(person) {
 console.log(person.name + " is " + person.age + " years old.");
});
```

This example uses the forEach method, which executes a function once for each item in the array. The function receives each item (in this case, an object) as an argument and can access its properties.

Each of these functionalities regarding arrays and objects are crucial for managing collections of data in JavaScript. Understanding how to manipulate these data structures is essential for handling complex data relationships and performing dynamic operations based on user input or external data sources.

Coding Exercises on Arrays and Objects

Arrays and Objects: Creating, accessing, and manipulating data structures. Here's a comprehensive set of coding exercises and multiple-choice quiz questions focused on arrays and objects in JavaScript, aiming to teach creation, access, and manipulation of these fundamental data structures.

Creating and Accessing an Array

Task: Create an array named colors with the elements "red", "blue", and "green". Print the second item in the array.
Purpose: Understand how to create arrays and access their elements.
Sample Code:
```
let colors = ["red", "blue", "green"];
console.log(colors[1]); // Outputs "blue"
```
Explanation:
This exercise involves creating an array using square brackets and accessing its elements using zero-based indexing. The element at index 1 (second element) of the colors array is "blue".

Adding and Removing Elements in an Array

Task: Start with an empty array named numbers. Add numbers 1 through 5 to the array using a loop, then remove the last element.

Purpose: Practice using methods to dynamically modify an array.

Sample Code:

```
let numbers = [];
for (let i = 1; i <= 5; i++) {
 numbers.push(i);
}
numbers.pop(); // Removes the last element
console.log(numbers); // Outputs [1, 2, 3, 4]
```

Explanation:

This code demonstrates using push() to add elements to the end of an array and pop() to remove the last element. The loop adds integers from 1 to 5, and pop() removes the last entry.

Creating and Accessing an Object

Task: Create an object named car with properties make, model, and year. Set them to "Toyota", "Corolla", and 2021, respectively. Print the model of the car.

Purpose: Learn how to create objects and access their properties.

Sample Code:

```
let car = {
 make: "Toyota",
 model: "Corolla",
 year: 2021
};
console.log(car.model); // Outputs "Corolla"
```

Explanation:

This exercise shows how to define an object using curly braces and key-value pairs. Properties of the object can be accessed using dot notation.

Updating Object Properties

Task: Given an object person with properties name and age, update age to 25 and add a new property job with the value "Engineer".

Purpose: Understand how to update and add properties to an object.

Sample Code:

```
let person = {
 name: "John Doe",
 age: 24
};
person.age = 25; // Update age
person.job = "Engineer"; // Add new property
console.log(person);
```

Explanation:

The person object is modified by directly assigning new values to its properties. This includes both updating an existing property and adding a new one.

Iterating Over an Array of Objects

Task: Create an array of objects where each object represents a book with a title and author. Use a loop to print each book's details.

Purpose: Practice iterating over complex data structures and accessing their properties.

Sample Code:

```
let books = [
  { title: "1984", author: "George Orwell" },
  { title: "The Great Gatsby", author: "F. Scott Fitzgerald" }
```

```
];
for (let book of books) {
  console.log(`Title: ${book.title}, Author: ${book.author}`);
}
```

Explanation:

This code creates an array containing multiple objects and uses a for...of loop to iterate through the array, accessing properties of each object.

Multiple Choice Quiz Questions

How do you access the first element of an array named fruits?

A) fruits[1]

B) fruits(0)

C) fruits[0]

D) fruits.first()

Correct Answer: C) fruits[0]

Explanation: Arrays in JavaScript are zero-indexed, so the first element is accessed using fruits[0].

What will the following code output?

let data = {a: 1, b: 2};

console.log(data['b']);

A) 1

B) 2

C) undefined

D) {b: 2}

Correct Answer: B) 2

Explanation: The code uses bracket notation to access the property b of the object data, which is set to 2.

Which method can be used to add an element at the beginning of an array?

A) push()

B) unshift()
C) append()
D) prepend()
Correct Answer: B) unshift()
Explanation: The unshift() method adds one or more elements to the beginning of an array and returns the new length of the array.

Given the following object, which operation will correctly change the year to 2022?
let vehicle = {type: "car", year: 2021};
A) vehicle.year = 2022;
B) vehicle.setYear(2022);
C) vehicle[year] = 2022;
D) vehicle['year'] = '2022';
Correct Answer: A) vehicle.year = 2022;
Explanation: The dot notation is correctly used to access and assign a new value to the year property of the vehicle object.

What does the pop() method do to an array?
A) Adds an element to the end of the array.
B) Removes the last element of the array and returns it.
C) Removes the first element of the array and returns it.
D) Checks if the array is empty.
Correct Answer: B) Removes the last element of the array and returns it.
Explanation: The pop() method removes the last element from an array and returns that element. This alters the length of the array.

These exercises and quiz questions provide a solid foundation for learning about arrays and objects in JavaScript, crucial for managing and manipulating collections of data in web development.

Advanced Functions

Let's dive into some of the more advanced aspects of functions in JavaScript. These include anonymous functions, arrow functions, closures, immediately invoked function expressions (IIFEs), and how arrow functions can be used to simplify code. Understanding these advanced concepts is crucial for efficient scripting and modern JavaScript development.

Anonymous Function
Anonymous functions are functions without a name. They are often not accessible after their initial creation and are commonly used in situations where functions are used as values.
Example: Using an Anonymous Function
```
let show = function() {
 console.log("Hello, this is an anonymous function.");
};
show(); // Calls the anonymous function
```
Here, the function is stored in the variable show, and it has no name between the function keyword and the parentheses.

Arrow Function
Introduced in ES6, arrow functions provide a concise syntax for writing functions. They are especially useful for short functions that just return a value. Arrow functions also don't bind their own this, making them ideal for use in contexts where you want to maintain the this value from the surrounding code.
Example: Basic Arrow Function
```
const add = (a, b) => a + b;
console.log(add(5, 3)); // Output: 8
```
This example shows a simple arrow function that takes two parameters and returns their sum. The return statement is omitted because the function consists of only one expression.

Closure
A closure is a function that remembers the variables from the place where it was defined, regardless of where it is executed later. They are useful for creating private variables or functions that can only be accessed through provided methods.

53

Example: Creating a Closure
```
function makeCounter() {
 let count = 0;
 return function() {
 return count++; // Accesses and modifies a variable from the
outer function
 };
}
let counter = makeCounter();
console.log(counter()); // Output: 0
console.log(counter()); // Output: 1
```
The counter function remembers the count variable from its surrounding scope, making count act like a private variable.

Immediately Invoked Function Expression (IIFE)

An IIFE is a function that runs as soon as it is defined. It is a design pattern which is also used to create a new scope, isolating the function from the global scope.
Example: Using an IIFE
```
(function() {
 let message = "IIFE Example";
 console.log(message);
})();
```
This function executes immediately upon its definition. The variables inside the IIFE (like message) do not pollute the global scope.

Using Arrow Function to Simplify Code

Arrow functions can make code cleaner and more readable, especially when dealing with functions that require only a single operation.
Example: Simplifying with Arrow Functions
```
let numbers = [1, 2, 3, 4, 5];
let squares = numbers.map(number => number * number); //
Uses arrow function
```

```
console.log(squares); // Output: [1, 4, 9, 16, 25]
```
Here, an arrow function is used with the map method to create a new array containing the squares of the numbers in the original array. This approach is much cleaner compared to using a traditional function expression.

Understanding these advanced functions enhances your ability to write more concise, efficient, and readable JavaScript code. These functions are particularly useful in modern JavaScript frameworks and libraries, where functional programming patterns are prevalent.

Coding Exercises on Advanced Functions in JavaScript

Advanced Functions: Anonymous functions, arrow functions, closures, and IIFEs (Immediately Invoked Function Expressions). Here's a comprehensive set of coding exercises and multiple-choice quiz questions focused on advanced functions in JavaScript, including anonymous functions, arrow functions, closures, and Immediately Invoked Function Expressions (IIFEs). These exercises are designed to deepen understanding of these advanced concepts through practical application and testing.

Anonymous Function

Task: Create an anonymous function assigned to a variable displayMessage that prints "Hello, JavaScript!" to the console.
Purpose: Understand how to define and use anonymous functions.
Sample Code:
```
let displayMessage = function() {
 console.log("Hello, JavaScript!");
};
displayMessage(); // Invocation of the anonymous function
```
Explanation:
This exercise involves defining an anonymous function (a function without a name) and assigning it to a variable. The function is then called using the variable name. This is a common pattern for creating encapsulated code blocks.

Arrow Function

Task: Rewrite the above anonymous function as an arrow function.

Purpose: Learn to use the concise syntax of arrow functions.

Sample Code:

```
let displayMessage = () => {
 console.log("Hello, JavaScript!");
};
displayMessage();
```

Explanation:

Arrow functions provide a shorter syntax for writing functions. They are especially useful for simple functions that contain a single statement, as shown in this example.

Closure

Task: Create a function createCounter that uses a closure to create a private variable count initialized at 0. The function should return another function that, when invoked, increments and prints the value of count.

Purpose: Explore closures to encapsulate and preserve data across multiple function calls.

Sample Code:

```
function createCounter() {
 let count = 0;
 return function() {
 count += 1;
 console.log(count);
 };
}
let myCounter = createCounter();
myCounter(); // Outputs 1
myCounter(); // Outputs 2
```

Explanation:

This exercise demonstrates how closures allow a function to have private variables. The count variable is accessible only within the scope of the closure but persists between function calls.

Immediately Invoked Function Expression (IIFE)

Task: Define an IIFE that prints "IIFE executed!" to the console.

Purpose: Learn how IIFEs are used to execute functions immediately as they are defined.

Sample Code:
```
(function() {
  console.log("IIFE executed!");
})();
```

Explanation:
An IIFE is a function that runs as soon as it is defined. It is defined using function syntax and immediately called using parentheses. This pattern is often used to isolate variables and avoid polluting the global scope.

Using Arrow Function to Simplify Code

Task: Write an arrow function that takes an array of numbers and returns a new array with each number doubled.

Purpose: Practice using arrow functions in conjunction with array methods like map.

Sample Code:
```
let doubleNumbers = numbers => numbers.map(number =>
number * 2);
console.log(doubleNumbers([1, 2, 3])); // Outputs [2, 4, 6]
```

Explanation:

This arrow function uses the map method to iterate over an array and apply a function to each element. The function to double a number is also written as an arrow function, showcasing a common practical use of arrow functions in JavaScript.

Multiple Choice Quiz Questions

What is an anonymous function in JavaScript?
A) A function named "anonymous"
B) A function without a defined name
C) A function assigned to a variable
D) A function that deletes itself after execution
Correct Answer: B) A function without a defined name
Explanation: Anonymous functions are functions that are defined without a name. They can be assigned to variables or used as function arguments.

Which feature is most associated with closures in JavaScript?
A) Preventing variables from being hoisted
B) Keeping variable values after the outer function has executed
C) Automatically destroying local variables
D) Passing arguments to functions without calling them
Correct Answer: B) Keeping variable values after the outer function has executed
Explanation: Closures are a powerful feature in JavaScript where an inner function has access to the outer (enclosing) function's variables, allowing it to retain and modify these variables between executions.

What does the following JavaScript code represent?
(() => console.log('Executed!'))();
A) Syntax error

B) A loop function

C) An IIFE

D) An object literal

Correct Answer: C) An IIFE

Explanation: This is an example of an arrow function being used as an Immediately Invoked Function Expression (IIFE), which is executed right after it's defined.

Which statement is true about arrow functions?

A) They have their own this context.

B) They cannot return values.

C) They are not suitable for methods that use this.

D) They can be used as constructors.

Correct Answer: C) They are not suitable for methods that use this.

Explanation: Arrow functions capture the this value of the enclosing context, so they are not suitable for defining object methods where its own this is expected.

How can you pass parameters to an IIFE?

A) (function(x, y) { return x + y; })(2, 3);

B) function(x, y) { return x + y; }(2, 3);

C) ((x, y) => { return x + y; })(2, 3);

D) All of the above

Correct Answer: D) All of the above

Explanation: All options correctly show how parameters can be passed to IIFEs, whether they are defined using traditional function syntax or arrow functions.

These exercises and questions provide a structured approach to mastering advanced function concepts in JavaScript, enhancing both practical coding skills and theoretical understanding.

Error Handling and Debugging

In JavaScript, robust error handling and debugging are essential for building reliable applications. Error handling mechanisms allow you to manage and respond to exceptions or errors that occur during execution, ensuring that your program can gracefully handle unexpected situations. Here, I'll explain the key concepts of error handling in JavaScript, including try...catch blocks, the finally clause, custom error throwing, nested try...catch blocks, and handling errors in asynchronous code.

Basic try...catch Implementation
The try...catch structure is used to handle exceptions that may occur in a block of code. The try block contains the code that might throw an exception, while the catch block contains code that executes if an exception occurs.
Example: Basic try...catch

```
try {
// Code that may throw an error
 console.log(undeclaredVariable); // This variable has not been
defined
} catch (error) {
 console.log("An error occurred:", error.message);
}
```

In this example, attempting to access undeclaredVariable throws a ReferenceError because it is not defined. The error is caught by the catch block, which then logs an error message.

Using finally Block
The finally block executes after the try and catch blocks have completed executing, regardless of whether an exception was thrown or caught. It is typically used to perform cleanup actions.
Example: Using finally

```
try {
 console.log("Try block executed.");
 throw new Error("Something went wrong!");
} catch (error) {
 console.log("Error caught:", error.message);
```

```
} finally {
  console.log("Finally block executed.");
}
```
Here, even though an error is thrown and caught, the finally block still executes, ensuring that any necessary cleanup or final steps are performed.

Throwing Custom Errors

You can throw custom errors using the throw statement. This is useful for creating specific error conditions in your code.
Example: Throwing Custom Errors
```
function checkAge(age) {
  if (age < 18) {
    throw new Error("Access denied - you are too young!");
  } else {
    console.log("Access granted.");
  }
}
try {
  checkAge(16);
} catch (error) {
  console.log("Caught an error:", error.message);
}
```
In this example, throw creates a new Error object with a custom message if the age condition is not met.

Nested try...catch Blocks

Nested try...catch blocks allow for handling errors in different parts of a complex function or during different stages of a process.
Example: Nested try...catch
```
try {
  console.log("Outer try block");
  try {
    throw new Error("Error in inner try");
  } catch (innerError) {
    console.log("Caught in inner catch:", innerError.message);
  }
} catch (outerError) {
  console.log("Caught in outer catch:", outerError.message);
} finally {
  console.log("Finally after outer try-catch");
```

```
}
```

This structure allows for inner blocks to handle specific errors while the outer blocks can catch any unhandled exceptions from the inner blocks or additional code segments.

Error Handling in Asynchronous Code

Error handling in asynchronous code can be more complex due to the nature of JavaScript's event loop. Common approaches include using promises with .catch() or async/await with try...catch.

Example: Error Handling with Async/Await

```
async function fetchData() {
  try {
  let response = await fetch('https://api.example.com/data');
  let data = await response.json();
  console.log(data);
  } catch (error) {
  console.log("An error occurred:", error.message);
  }
}
fetchData();
```

In this example, fetchData is an asynchronous function that attempts to fetch data from a URL. The try...catch block here catches any errors that might occur during the fetch operation or when converting the response to JSON, such as network errors or invalid JSON.

Understanding and implementing effective error handling in JavaScript can significantly improve the reliability and user experience of your applications, ensuring they operate smoothly even when facing unexpected conditions.

Coding Exercises on JavaScript Error Handling and Debugging

Error Handling and Debugging: try, catch, finally blocks, throwing custom errors, and using debugging tools. Here's a comprehensive set of coding exercises and multiple-choice quiz questions focused on error handling and debugging in JavaScript. This includes using try, catch, finally blocks, throwing custom errors, and utilizing debugging tools to identify and resolve issues.

To have the fetchData function work locally with a data file, you'll first need to create a JSON file that contains the data you want to fetch. Then, you'll serve this file using a local server since fetch is designed to work over HTTP and accessing local files directly with fetch could lead to CORS (Cross-Origin Resource Sharing) issues or fetch simply not working due to browser security restrictions.

Here's how you can set up and use a local environment for testing your fetchData function:

Create a JSON file (let's call it data.json) and put some sample data into it. Here's an example of what this file could look like:

```
{
   "users": [
      {"id": 1, "name": "Alice"},
      {"id": 2, "name": "Bob"}
   ]
}
```

Update Your fetchData Function to Use the Local URL. In my case I am using port 5500 on my local server.
fetchData("http://127.0.0.1:5500/data.json");

Basic try...catch Implementation

Task: Write a JavaScript function that attempts to parse a JSON string and uses try...catch to handle any errors that arise.
Purpose: Understand how to catch and handle errors gracefully in a controlled manner.
Sample Code:

```
function parseJSON(jsonString) {
try {
let jsonObj = JSON.parse(jsonString);
console.log("JSON parsed successfully:", jsonObj);
} catch (error) {
console.error("Failed to parse JSON:", error);
}
}
parseJSON('{"name":"John", "age":30}'); // Valid JSON
parseJSON('{"name": "John", "age": 30'); // Invalid JSON
```

Explanation:
This code tries to parse a JSON string. If the JSON is valid, it logs the parsed object. If parsing fails (e.g., due to syntax errors), the error is caught by the catch block, which then logs an error message.

Using finally Block

Task: Implement a finally block that runs after try...catch to clean up resources, regardless of whether an error occurred.
Purpose: Demonstrate the use of finally to perform cleanup activities.
Sample Code:

```
function loadData(url) {
try {
// Simulate loading data
console.log(`Loading data from ${url}`);
throw new Error("Network error");
} catch (error) {
```

```
console.error("An error occurred:", error.message);
} finally {
console.log("Cleanup actions completed");
}
}
loadData("https://api.example.com/data");
```
Explanation:
In this example, the finally block executes after the try and catch blocks, ensuring that cleanup code runs regardless of whether an error occurred during the data loading process.

Throwing Custom Errors

Task: Write a function that checks the age parameter and throws a custom error if the age is less than 18.
Purpose: Practice throwing custom errors based on specific conditions.
Sample Code:
```
function verifyAge(age) {
try {
if (age < 18) {
throw new Error("You must be 18 years or older.");
}
console.log("Age verified:", age);
} catch (error) {
console.error("Verification failed:", error.message);
}
}
verifyAge(21); // Passes verification
verifyAge(16); // Fails verification
```
Explanation:
This function uses a conditional check within a try block to throw a custom error if the age is below 18. The catch block handles this error by logging an appropriate message.

Nested try...catch Blocks

Task: Utilize nested try...catch blocks to handle different types of errors in complex code sections.

Purpose: Show how nested try...catch structures can be used to differentiate error handling strategies.

Sample Code:

```javascript
function processFile(data) {
try {
console.log("Processing data...");
try {
let result = JSON.parse(data);
console.log("Data processed:", result);
} catch (parseError) {
throw new Error("Data parsing failed.");
}
} catch (error) {
console.error("Error:", error.message);
}
}
processFile('{"valid": "json"}');
processFile('invalid json');
```

Explanation:

The outer try block handles broader processing tasks, while the inner try block specifically attempts to parse JSON data, each with its own error handling logic.

Error Handling in Asynchronous Code

Task: Use try...catch within an asynchronous function to handle errors in promises.

Purpose: Explore error handling in asynchronous operations using async/await.

Sample Code:

```javascript
async function fetchData(url) {
try {
```

```
let response = await fetch(url);
let data = await response.json();
console.log("Data fetched successfully:", data);
} catch (error) {
console.error("Failed to fetch data:", error);
}
}
fetchData("https://api.example.com/data");
```

Explanation:

This asynchronous function attempts to fetch data from a URL and parse it as JSON. If either the network request or the parsing fails, the error is caught and handled in the catch block.

Multiple Choice Quiz Questions

What does the catch block do in a try...catch statement?
A) Executes a function if no errors were thrown in the try block
B) Catches and handles any errors thrown in the try block
C) Displays all errors as alerts in the browser
D) Sends errors to external logging services
Correct Answer: B) Catches and handles any errors thrown in the try block
Explanation: The catch block is designed to intercept and handle any errors that occur within the preceding try block, allowing for graceful error handling.

What is the purpose of the finally block in error handling?
A) To throw any unhandled errors
B) To perform clean-up operations after executing the try and catch blocks
C) To execute additional try blocks
D) To handle errors instead of the catch block
Correct Answer: B) To perform clean-up operations after executing the try and catch blocks

Explanation: The finally block is used to execute code after the try and catch blocks have completed, regardless of whether an error was caught.

What will happen if you throw an error without a catch block to handle it?

A) The error will be ignored
B) The error will be logged in the console automatically
C) The program will continue execution normally
D) The error will cause the program to terminate or the script to stop executing
Correct Answer: D) The error will cause the program to terminate or the script to stop executing
Explanation: Throwing an error without a corresponding catch block to handle it will result in the script stopping execution, potentially causing the program to terminate.

Which of the following is true about custom errors in JavaScript?

A) They cannot be caught by catch blocks
B) They are only for displaying errors and cannot contain logic
C) They can be used to create specific error types and messages
D) They are automatically logged to external systems
Correct Answer: C) They can be used to create specific error types and messages
Explanation: Custom errors allow developers to throw specific error types with custom messages, enhancing error handling by making it easier to understand and manage the errors that occur.

How should you handle errors in asynchronous code that uses promises?

A) Errors in promises cannot be caught
B) Use a catch method chained to the promise
C) Errors in promises are automatically handled by the browser
D) Use a timeout to catch errors

Correct Answer: B) Use a catch method chained to the promise
Explanation: Errors in promises should be handled using the catch method chained to the promise or within a try...catch block in an async function, ensuring that errors are caught and managed appropriately.

These exercises and questions provide a thorough understanding of handling errors and debugging in JavaScript, crucial for developing robust and error-resistant applications.

Introduction to the DOM

The Document Object Model (DOM) is a programming interface for web documents. It represents the page so that programs can change the document structure, style, and content. The DOM represents the document as nodes and objects; this way, programming languages can interact with the page.

JavaScript can be used to manipulate the DOM, which allows scripts to dynamically change document content, structure, and styles, adding a lot of interactivity to a site. Below, I'll explain key concepts of DOM manipulation including selecting elements, creating and appending elements, modifying styles, handling events, and removing elements.

Selecting Elements
To manipulate an element on the web page, you first need to select it. JavaScript provides several methods to select elements from the DOM.
Example: Selecting Elements
let elementById = document.getElementById('myElement'); // Selects an element by its ID
let elementsByClass = document.getElementsByClassName('myClass'); // Selects all elements with a specific class
let elementsByTag = document.getElementsByTagName('div'); // Selects all <div> elements
let elementByQuery = document.querySelector('.myClass'); // Selects the first element matching the CSS query
let allElementsByQuery = document.querySelectorAll('.myClass'); // Selects all elements matching the CSS query
These functions allow you to access DOM elements to manipulate them, such as changing their properties or contents.

Creating and Appending Elements
You can create new elements in the DOM and append them to existing elements.
Example: Creating and Appending Elements

```
let newDiv = document.createElement('div'); // Creates a new
<div> element
let newText = document.createTextNode('Hello World'); //
Creates a text node
newDiv.appendChild(newText); // Appends the text node to
the newly created <div>
document.body.appendChild(newDiv); // Appends the <div>
to the body of the document
```
This example shows how to create a new <div> element, add text to it, and then append it to the <body> of the document.

Modifying Styles
DOM manipulation also allows you to change the styling of elements dynamically.
Example: Modifying Styles
```
let element = document.getElementById('myElement');
element.style.color = 'red'; // Changes the text color of the
element
element.style.backgroundColor = 'blue'; // Changes the
background color of the element
```
This code accesses an element by its ID and changes its text color and background color.

Event Handling
Events are actions that can be detected by your web application, such as clicks, key presses, or page loads. JavaScript can react to these events using event listeners.
Example: Event Handling
```
let button = document.getElementById('myButton');
button.addEventListener('click', function() {
 alert('Button was clicked!');
});
```
This sets up an event listener on a button, so when the button is clicked, it triggers an alert.

Removing Elements
Finally, you might find situations where you need to remove elements from the DOM.
Example: Removing Elements
```
let elementToRemove =
document.getElementById('removeMe');
```

elementToRemove.parentNode.removeChild(elementToRemo
ve);
This finds an element and removes it from the DOM. It's
necessary to access the parent node to remove the target
element, as DOM nodes can only be removed by their parent.

These examples cover fundamental techniques for interacting
with the DOM using JavaScript. By mastering these, you can
begin to build highly interactive and dynamic web applications.

Coding Exercises on JavaScript and the DOM

**Introduction to the DOM: What is the DOM, and how
JavaScript interacts with it.** Here's a structured set of coding
exercises and multiple-choice quiz questions focused on the
Document Object Model (DOM) in JavaScript. These are
designed to help learners understand what the DOM is and
how JavaScript can interact with it to manipulate web pages
dynamically.

Selecting Elements

Task: Use JavaScript to select an HTML element with the ID
title and change its text to "Hello, DOM!".
Purpose: Learn how to select elements and modify their
content.
HTML + JavaScript Code:

```
<h1 id="title">Original Title</h1>
<script>
 let titleElement = document.getElementById('title');
 titleElement.textContent = "Hello, DOM!";
</script>
```

Explanation:

This exercise shows how to select a DOM element using getElementById, a method that retrieves an element by its ID. The textContent property is then used to change the text of the selected element.

Creating and Appending Elements

Task: Create a new div element, add some text to it, and append it to the body of the document.
Purpose: Practice creating elements and appending them to the DOM.
HTML + JavaScript Code:

```
<script>
 let newDiv = document.createElement('div');
 newDiv.textContent = "Added a new div!";
 document.body.appendChild(newDiv);
</script>
```

Explanation:
This code demonstrates how to create a new DOM element using createElement, set its text content, and then append it to the document body using appendChild. This method is fundamental for dynamically adding content to a web page.

Modifying Styles

Task: Select a paragraph element by its class description and change its color to blue.
Purpose: Understand how to manipulate CSS styles through JavaScript.
HTML + JavaScript Code:

```
<p class="description">This is a description paragraph.</p>
<script>
 let para = document.querySelector('.description');
 para.style.color = 'blue';
</script>
```

Explanation:
This exercise uses querySelector to select the first element that matches the specified CSS selector. The style property is then used to change the color of the text to blue.

Event Handling

Task: Attach an event listener to a button that logs "Button clicked" to the console when it is clicked.
Purpose: Learn to interact with DOM elements using events.
HTML + JavaScript Code:

```
<button id="myButton">Click me</button>
<script>

document.getElementById('myButton').addEventListener('click', function() {
console.log("Button clicked");
});
</script>
```

Explanation:
This code adds an event listener to a button. The addEventListener method is crucial for handling user interactions, allowing functions to be executed in response to certain events like clicks.

Removing Elements

Task: Remove an element with the ID remove-me from the document.
Purpose: Understand how to remove elements from the DOM.
HTML + JavaScript Code:

```
<div id="remove-me">Remove this div</div>
<script>
```

```
let removeElement = document.getElementById('remove-
me');
 removeElement.parentNode.removeChild(removeElement);
</script>
```
Explanation:

This script selects an element and removes it from the DOM using removeChild. This method requires calling removeChild on the parent node of the element to be removed, illustrating the hierarchical nature of the DOM.

Multiple Choice Quiz Questions

What is the DOM in web development?

A) A programming interface for web documents

B) A type of web server

C) A database of web pages

D) A JavaScript framework

Correct Answer: A) A programming interface for web documents

Explanation: The DOM (Document Object Model) is a programming interface that allows programs and scripts to dynamically access and update the content, structure, and style of a document.

Which method can be used to select a single element by its ID?

A) document.findElementById()

B) document.getElementById()

C) document.querySelector()

D) document.getElement()

Correct Answer: B) document.getElementById()

Explanation: document.getElementById() is a DOM method specifically designed to select a single element by its ID attribute.

How can JavaScript directly change the style of an HTML element?

A) By editing the element's style attribute in the HTML file

B) By using the style property in JavaScript

C) By changing the CSS file linked to the HTML

D) JavaScript cannot change styles directly

Correct Answer: B) By using the style property in JavaScript

Explanation: The style property of a DOM element in JavaScript can be used to get or set the inline style of an element.

What is the correct way to add a new element to the DOM?

A) document.createElement('div').add()

B) document.appendChild(document.createElement('div'))

C)
document.body.appendChild(document.createElement('div'))

D) document.create('div').appendTo(body)

Correct Answer: C)
document.body.appendChild(document.createElement('div'))

Explanation: To add a new element to the DOM, you first create the element using document.createElement() and then append it to an existing DOM node using appendChild(), such as document.body.

Which JavaScript method is used to add an event listener that specifies a function to execute when a specific event occurs on an element?

A) document.onEvent()

B) document.addEventListener()

C) document.eventHandler()

D) document.bindEvent()

Correct Answer: B) document.addEventListener()

Explanation: document.addEventListener() is used to attach an event handler to the document or any element within the document. It allows you to specify the type of event and the function to execute when that event occurs.

These exercises and questions provide a foundational understanding of how the DOM works and how JavaScript can be used to manipulate it, key skills for any web developer.

Manipulating the DOM

In JavaScript, manipulating the Document Object Model (DOM) is essential for creating interactive web applications. The DOM provides a structured representation of the document (such as HTML) and defines ways in which structures can be accessed and manipulated. Below, I'll discuss several key DOM manipulation techniques: selecting elements and changing their content, creating and appending elements, removing elements, modifying element styles, and handling events on dynamically created elements.

Selecting Elements and Changing Content

To manipulate elements, you first need to select them. Once selected, you can change their content, attributes, and more.
Example: Selecting Elements and Changing Content
const heading = document.getElementById('heading'); // Selects the element with id 'heading'
heading.textContent = 'New Heading Text'; // Changes the text content of the selected element

- document.getElementById is a method that retrieves an element by its ID.
- textContent is a property that sets or returns the text content of the specified node and its descendants.

Creating and Appending an Element

Creating new elements and appending them to the DOM is a common task, especially when dynamically generating content like lists, tables, or other structured data.
Example: Creating and Appending an Element
const newParagraph = document.createElement('p'); // Creates a new paragraph element
newParagraph.textContent = 'This is a new paragraph'; // Sets the text content of the paragraph
document.body.appendChild(newParagraph); // Appends the new paragraph to the body of the document

- document.createElement creates a new element of the specified type.

- appendChild adds a node to the end of the list of children of a specified parent node.

Removing an Element
Removing elements from the DOM is straightforward once you have a reference to the element and its parent.
Example: Removing an Element
const oldParagraph =
document.getElementById('oldParagraph'); // Selects the element with id 'oldParagraph'
oldParagraph.parentNode.removeChild(oldParagraph); // Removes the selected element from its parent

- parentNode returns the parent node of the specified element.
- removeChild removes a child node from the DOM.

Modifying Element Styles
Changing the styles of elements dynamically allows you to create interactive and responsive UIs.
Example: Modifying Element Styles
const element = document.getElementById('myElement');
element.style.backgroundColor = 'blue'; // Changes the background color of the element
element.style.color = 'white'; // Changes the text color of the element
element.style.padding = '10px'; // Adds padding to the element

- The style property accesses the style object of an element, which corresponds to the inline styles of that element.

Event Handling on Dynamically Created Elements
Handling events on elements that are created dynamically (i.e., after the initial page load) can be challenging due to how events are bound to elements.
Example: Event Handling on Dynamically Created Elements
document.body.addEventListener('click', function(event) {
if (event.target.tagName === 'BUTTON') {
alert('Button clicked!');
}
});

- This uses event delegation by adding an event listener to a parent element (in this case, the body).
- event.target checks if the clicked element is a button, ensuring that the event handler responds appropriately even if the button was added after this script was executed.

These examples illustrate basic but powerful ways to manipulate the DOM using JavaScript. By understanding and using these methods, you can start to build more interactive and dynamic web applications.

Coding Exercises on Manipulating the DOM

Manipulating the DOM: Selecting elements, changing content, creating, and removing elements. Here's a collection of coding exercises and multiple-choice quiz questions focused on manipulating the Document Object Model (DOM) in JavaScript. These exercises will guide learners through selecting elements, changing content, creating new elements, and removing existing ones.

Selecting Elements and Changing Content

Task: Use JavaScript to select a paragraph with the class info and change its text to "Updated content here!".
Purpose: Practice selecting elements by class and modifying their content.
HTML + JavaScript Code:

```
<p class="info">Original content</p>
<script>
let paragraph = document.querySelector('.info');
paragraph.textContent = "Updated content here!";
</script>
```

Explanation:

This exercise demonstrates the use of querySelector to select the first element that matches a specified CSS selector (.info). The textContent property is then used to change the text inside the paragraph.

Creating and Appending an Element

Task: Create a new li element, add text to it, and append it to an existing ul with the ID myList.

Purpose: Learn to dynamically create elements and append them to existing structures.

HTML + JavaScript Code:

```
<ul id="myList">
 <li>Item 1</li>
 <li>Item 2</li>
</ul>
<script>
 let newItem = document.createElement('li');
 newItem.textContent = "Item 3";
 document.getElementById('myList').appendChild(newItem);
</script>
```

Explanation:

In this example, createElement is used to create a new li element. The textContent property is used to add text to the new element. Finally, appendChild is used to add this new element to the end of the ul identified by myList.

Removing an Element

Task: Remove the first li element from the list with the ID myList.

Purpose: Practice removing elements from the DOM.

HTML + JavaScript Code:

```
<ul id="myList">
```

```
<li>Item 1</li>
<li>Item 2</li>
<li>Item 3</li>
</ul>
<script>
let list = document.getElementById('myList');
let firstItem = list.querySelector('li'); // Selects the first li
list.removeChild(firstItem);
</script>
```

Explanation:

This script selects the first li element within the ul using querySelector and removes it using removeChild. This method removes a child node from the DOM, allowing for dynamic modifications to page content.

Modifying Element Styles

Task: Change the color and font size of all paragraphs on the page.

Purpose. Utilize JavaScript to modify CSS properties of DOM elements.

HTML + JavaScript Code:

```
<p>First paragraph.</p>
<p>Second paragraph.</p>
<script>
let paragraphs = document.querySelectorAll('p');
paragraphs.forEach(p => {
p.style.color = 'blue';
p.style.fontSize = '18px';
});
</script>
```

Explanation:

querySelectorAll selects all paragraph elements on the page. The forEach method is used to apply style changes to each paragraph, demonstrating how to manipulate multiple elements at once.

Event Handling on Dynamically Created Elements

Task: Add a button that, when clicked, adds a new item to the list. Each item should have a click event that alerts its text when clicked.

Purpose: Combine element creation and event handling in a dynamic context.

HTML + JavaScript Code:

```
<button id="addButton">Add Item</button>
<ul id="myList">
 <li>Item 1</li>
 <li>Item 2</li>
</ul>
<script>

document.getElementById('addButton').addEventListener('click', function() {
 let newItem = document.createElement('li');
 newItem.textContent = `Item ${document.querySelectorAll('#myList li').length + 1}`;
 newItem.onclick = function() { alert(this.textContent); };
 document.getElementById('myList').appendChild(newItem);
});
</script>
```

Explanation:

This script adds an event listener to a button that creates a new li element each time it's clicked, appends it to the ul, and assigns an onclick event that alerts the item's content. It shows how to handle events on elements created dynamically.

Multiple Choice Quiz Questions

Which method is best suited for selecting a single element with a specific ID?

A) document.querySelector()

B) document.getElementById()

C) document.getElementsByClassName()

D) document.getElementsByTagName()

Correct Answer: B) document.getElementById()

Explanation: While document.querySelector() can also select elements by ID, document.getElementById() is specifically designed for this purpose and is more efficient.

What does the createElement function do in JavaScript?

A) Changes an existing element's tag name

B) Creates a new DOM element of the specified type

C) Modifies the content of an existing element

D) Finds elements of a specific type

Correct Answer: B) Creates a new DOM element of the specified type

Explanation: createElement is used to create a new element in the document, which can then be inserted into the DOM.

How can you remove an element from the DOM?

A) element.delete()

B) element.remove()

C) element.removeChild()

D) element.destroy()

Correct Answer: B) element.remove()

Explanation: element.remove() removes the element it is called on from the document. element.removeChild() is also valid but requires calling it on the parent of the element to be removed.

What property would you use to change the text inside an element?

A) innerHTML

B) textContent

C) innerText

D) Both A and B are correct

Correct Answer: D) Both A and B are correct

Explanation: Both innerHTML and textContent can be used to change the text inside an element, but innerHTML allows HTML markup, whereas textContent changes the text only.

Which method is used to add a style directly to an HTML element in JavaScript?

A) element.style()

B) element.setStyle()

C) element.css()

D) element.style

Correct Answer: D) element.style

Explanation: The style property of a DOM element is used to get or set the inline style of that element, making it possible to change styles dynamically via JavaScript.

These exercises and questions provide a comprehensive introduction to DOM manipulation, a crucial skill for interactive web development.

Event Handling

Handling DOM events is crucial for interactive web applications. Events are actions or occurrences that happen in the system you are programming, which the system tells you about so your software can respond to them in some way. Below, I'll explain the JavaScript code and concepts used to handle different types of DOM events including mouse clicks, mouseovers, mouse outs, keyboard presses, form submissions, and changes in select elements.

Mouse Click Event

A mouse click event is triggered when the user clicks on an element. The most common type of click event is the click event.

Example: Handling a Mouse Click Event

```
const button = document.getElementById('myButton');
button.addEventListener('click', function() {
 alert('Button was clicked!');
});
```

- addEventListener is used to attach a click event handler to the button.
- When the button is clicked, the callback function is executed, triggering an alert.

Mouse Over and Mouse Out Events

Mouse over (mouseover) and mouse out (mouseout) events are triggered when the mouse pointer enters or leaves the element area respectively.

Example: Handling Mouse Over and Mouse Out Events

```
const box = document.getElementById('myBox');
box.addEventListener('mouseover', function() {
 box.style.backgroundColor = 'blue'; // Changes background color when mouse over
});
box.addEventListener('mouseout', function() {
 box.style.backgroundColor = 'red'; // Changes background color when mouse out
});
```

- The mouseover event changes the box's background color to blue when the mouse pointer is over the box.
- The mouseout event changes it back to red when the mouse pointer leaves the box.

Keyboard Event: Key Press

Keyboard events are triggered by user interactions with keyboard keys. The keypress event is deprecated and has been replaced by the keydown and keyup events for better support.

Example: Handling Keyboard Events

```
document.addEventListener('keydown', function(event) {
 console.log(`Key pressed: ${event.key}`); // Displays the pressed key
});
```

- This event handler listens for any key being pressed down on the keyboard.

- event.key provides the value of the key that was pressed.

Form Submit Event

The form submit event is triggered when a form is submitted.
Example: Handling Form Submit Event

```
const form = document.getElementById('myForm');
form.addEventListener('submit', function(event) {
 event.preventDefault(); // Prevents the default form
submission to the server
 alert('Form submitted!');
});
```

- This code prevents the default form submission behavior with preventDefault(), allowing for custom handling, such as validation or manual data submission via AJAX.

Change Event on Select Element

The change event on a select element is triggered when the user changes the selection.
Example: Handling Change Event on Select Element

```
const select = document.getElementById('mySelect');
select.addEventListener('change', function() {
 alert(`Option selected: ${select.value}`);
});
```

- This code sets up an event listener for the change event on a select dropdown.
- When the user selects a different option, the event triggers, and the alert displays the new selected value.

These examples illustrate handling various DOM events in JavaScript, enhancing the interactive capabilities of web pages by responding to user inputs and actions. Each type of event has specific use cases and can be managed with appropriate event listeners and handlers.

Coding Exercises on JavaScript Event Handling

Event Handling: Adding event listeners, event propagation, default actions, and handling events with JavaScript. Here's a detailed set of coding exercises and multiple-choice quiz questions focusing on event handling in JavaScript. These exercises will cover adding event listeners, understanding event propagation, preventing default actions, and using JavaScript to handle different events effectively.

Adding an Event Listener

Task: Create a button in HTML and add an event listener in JavaScript that alerts "Button clicked!" when the button is clicked.

Purpose: Learn to attach event listeners to HTML elements.

HTML + JavaScript Code:

```
<!-- HTML to create a button -->
<button id="myButton">Click Me</button>
<!-- JavaScript to add event listener -->
<script>

document.getElementById('myButton').addEventListener('click', function() {
  alert('Button clicked!');
});
</script>
```

Explanation:

This code adds an event listener to a button with the ID myButton. The addEventListener method is used to listen for the 'click' event, and it triggers a function that displays an alert.

Event Propagation (Bubbling and Capturing)

Task: Create a nested structure with a div containing a button. Demonstrate stopping the bubbling phase using stopPropagation.

Purpose: Understand how event propagation works and how to stop it.

HTML + JavaScript Code:

```
<div id="myDiv" style="padding: 20px; border: 1px solid black;">
 Click the box or the button!
 <button id="myButton">Click Me</button>
</div>
<script>
 document.getElementById('myDiv').addEventListener('click', function() {
 alert('Div clicked!');
 });

 document.getElementById('myButton').addEventListener('click', function(event) {
 event.stopPropagation();
 alert('Button clicked!');
 });
</script>
```

Explanation:

In this setup, clicking the button will alert "Button clicked!" and stop further propagation of the event, so the div's click event will not be triggered. This demonstrates the control of event flow using stopPropagation.

Preventing Default Actions

Task: Add an event listener to a link and prevent its default navigation action.

89

Purpose: Learn to prevent the default action of an event.
HTML + JavaScript Code:

```
<a href="https://www.example.com" id="myLink">Go to
Example.com</a>
<script>
document.getElementById('myLink').addEventListener('click',
function(event) {
event.preventDefault();
alert('Default action prevented!');
});
</script>
```

Explanation:
The event listener attached to the link intercepts the click event
and uses preventDefault to stop the link from navigating to
"https://www.example.com", displaying an alert instead.

Using this in Event Handlers

Task: Attach an event listener to multiple buttons that changes
their text to "Clicked" when they are clicked.
Purpose: Practice using this to refer to the event target within
an event handler.
HTML + JavaScript Code:

```
<button class="clickButton">Button 1</button>
<button class="clickButton">Button 2</button>
<script>
let buttons = document.querySelectorAll('.clickButton');
buttons.forEach(button => {
button.addEventListener('click', function() {
this.textContent = 'Clicked';
});
});
</script>
```

Explanation:

This code selects all buttons with the class clickButton and adds an event listener to each. Using this in the event handler refers to the button that was clicked, allowing the text to be changed dynamically.

Event Delegation

Task: Implement event delegation by adding a single event listener to a parent element that manages clicks for multiple child elements.
Purpose: Optimize event handling with event delegation.
HTML + JavaScript Code:

```
<ul id="myList">
 <li>Item 1</li>
 <li>Item 2</li>
 <li>Item 3</li>
</ul>
<script>
 document.getElementById('myList').addEventListener('click',
 function(event) {
 if (event.target.tagName === 'LI') {
 alert('You clicked on ' + event.target.textContent);
 }
 });
</script>
```

Explanation:
Instead of adding an event listener to each list item, a single listener on the parent ul element handles all clicks on its child li elements. This is a more memory-efficient approach, particularly for large lists.

Multiple Choice Quiz Questions

What does the addEventListener method do in JavaScript?
A) Changes the HTML content of an element

B) Adds a new HTML attribute to an element
C) Attaches an event handler to an element
D) Removes an existing event handler from an element
Correct Answer: C) Attaches an event handler to an element
Explanation: addEventListener is used to attach an event handler to a DOM element, which will listen for specific types of events and execute a function when those events occur.

What is event propagation in JavaScript?
A) The method of passing arguments to events
B) The way events sequence through phases including capturing and bubbling
C) The process of adding multiple event listeners to an element
D) The default action of reloading the page when an event occurs
Correct Answer: B) The way events sequence through phases including capturing and bubbling
Explanation: Event propagation refers to the way some events will travel from the window object down to the target element (capturing phase) and then back up to the window object (bubbling phase).

What method is used to prevent a form from submitting traditionally when a submit button is clicked?
A) stopPropagation()
B) preventDefault()
C) stopImmediatePropagation()
D) haltExecution()
Correct Answer: B) preventDefault()
Explanation: The preventDefault method is commonly used to prevent the default action of events, such as preventing a form from submitting in the traditional way when using AJAX to handle the form data.

In the context of event handling, what does the this keyword refer to within an event handler function?

A) The document object

B) The window object

C) The element that the event was attached to

D) The element that triggered the event

Correct Answer: C) The element that the event was attached to

Explanation: In event handlers, this refers to the element to which the event handler was attached, not necessarily the element that triggered the event.

Which technique is best for adding event listeners to a large number of similar elements?

A) Adding an event listener to each element individually

B) Using the window.onload event to add listeners

C) Adding a single event listener to their common parent element

D) Creating a loop to add listeners during page load

Correct Answer: C) Adding a single event listener to their common parent element

Explanation: Event delegation, by adding a single event listener to a common parent element, is more memory-efficient and performant, especially for handling events on large numbers of elements.

These exercises and questions provide a robust understanding of handling events in JavaScript, essential for interactive web development.

Handling DOM Events

Handling DOM Events: Interaction with mouse events, keyboard events, and form events. Here's a detailed set of coding exercises and multiple-choice quiz questions focused on handling DOM events in JavaScript. These exercises will help learners interact with various types of events including mouse events, keyboard events, and form events.

Coding Exercises on Handling DOM Events

Mouse Click Event

Task: Attach a click event listener to a button that changes the text of the button when it's clicked.
Purpose: Understand how to handle mouse click events.
HTML + JavaScript Code:

```
<button id="clickButton">Click me</button>
<script>

document.getElementById('clickButton').addEventListener('click', function() {
  this.textContent = "Clicked!";
});
</script>
```

Explanation:
This exercise shows how to use the addEventListener method to handle a click event on a button. When the button is clicked, the text content of the button is changed to "Clicked!", demonstrating a basic interaction.

Mouse Over and Mouse Out Events

Task: Attach mouseover and mouseout events to a div that change the div's color when the mouse hovers over it and reverts it when the mouse leaves.

Purpose: Practice using mouse event types to create interactive effects.

HTML + JavaScript Code:

```
<div id="hoverDiv" style="width: 200px; height: 200px;
background-color: blue;"></div>
<script>
let hoverDiv = document.getElementById('hoverDiv');
hoverDiv.addEventListener('mouseover', function() {
this.style.backgroundColor = 'red';
});
hoverDiv.addEventListener('mouseout', function() {
this.style.backgroundColor = 'blue';
});
</script>
```

Explanation:

This script adds two event listeners to a div: one for mouseover that changes the background color to red when the mouse hovers over the div, and one for mouseout that changes it back to blue when the mouse leaves.

Keyboard Event: Key Press

Task: Detect when the 'Enter' key is pressed and display an alert.

Purpose: Learn how to respond to keyboard events.

HTML + JavaScript Code:

```
<input type="text" id="inputBox" placeholder="Press 'Enter'
key">
<script>
```

```
document.getElementById('inputBox').addEventListener('keypr
ess', function(event) {
 if (event.key === 'Enter') {
 alert("Enter key pressed!");
 }
 });
</script>
```

Explanation:

The keypress event listener is attached to an input box. It uses the event object to check if the key pressed is the 'Enter' key, and if so, it triggers an alert.

Form Submit Event

Task: Handle the form submission event to prevent the default form submission and display form data in a div.

Purpose: Manipulate form behavior with JavaScript and handle data entry.

HTML + JavaScript Code:

```
<form id="myForm">
 <input type="text" name="username" placeholder="Enter
your name">
 <button type="submit">Submit</button>
</form>
<div id="result"></div>
<script>

document.getElementById('myForm').addEventListener('submi
t', function(event) {
 event.preventDefault();
 let name = this.elements['username'].value;
 document.getElementById('result').textContent = "Hello, " +
name;
 });
```

```
</script>
```

Explanation:

This code prevents the default submission of a form, which stops the page from reloading. It then takes the name entered into the form, and displays it in a div, demonstrating basic form handling and DOM manipulation.

Change Event on Select Element

Task: Attach a change event listener to a dropdown (select element) that updates a paragraph with the user's selection.
Purpose: Use the change event to act on user selections from a dropdown menu.
HTML + JavaScript Code:

```
<select id="mySelect">
 <option value="Apple">Apple</option>
 <option value="Banana">Banana</option>
 <option value="Cherry">Cherry</option>
</select>
<p id="selectedFruit">Selected fruit will appear here</p>
<script>

document.getElementById('mySelect').addEventListener('change', function() {
 let selectedValue = this.value;
 document.getElementById('selectedFruit').textContent = "You selected: " + selectedValue;
 });
</script>
```

Explanation:

When a user selects an option from the dropdown menu, the change event is fired. The event listener then updates a paragraph element to display the selected option, showing real-time interaction with user input.

Multiple Choice Quiz Questions

What does the event.preventDefault() method do when called inside an event handler function?
A) It stops the browser from executing the default action associated with the event.
B) It prevents the event from propagating or bubbling up to parent elements.
C) It cancels the event entirely, not allowing other handlers to execute.
D) It resets the event's default properties.
Correct Answer: A) It stops the browser from executing the default action associated with the event.
Explanation: event.preventDefault() is used to prevent the default action the browser takes on that event, such as following a link in <a href="...">.

Which event type would you use to detect when a user moves the mouse over an element?
A) click
B) mouseover
C) mousemove
D) mouseenter
Correct Answer: B) mouseover
Explanation: The mouseover event is triggered when the mouse pointer enters the element and its descendants. mouseenter is also a valid answer but is not listed as an option here.

How can you attach an event listener that runs only once?
A) Use the addEventListener method with the { once: true } option.
B) Remove the event listener manually inside the handler.
C) Use the one method instead of addEventListener.
D) Set a global variable to track if the event has run.

Correct Answer: A) Use the addEventListener method with the { once: true } option.

Explanation: The { once: true } option for addEventListener allows the event to be executed only once per element per event type.

Which keyboard event can detect when a user presses the escape key?
A) keypress
B) keyup
C) keydown
D) Both B and C
Correct Answer: D) Both B and C

Explanation: Both keyup and keydown can detect all individual key presses, including the escape key. keypress is deprecated and doesn't register keys like escape.

What is the difference between change and input events for an <input> element?
A) change fires during the input, input fires after the element loses focus.
B) change fires after the element loses focus if the value has changed, input fires immediately upon value change.
C) There is no difference; both events are interchangeable.
D) change is for checkboxes and radio buttons, input is for text fields.
Correct Answer: B) change fires after the element loses focus if the value has changed, input fires immediately upon value change.

Explanation: The input event occurs immediately when the value of an <input>, <select>, or <textarea> element is changed. In contrast, the change event triggers after the element loses focus, provided the value has changed.

These exercises and quiz questions offer a practical understanding of handling various DOM events in JavaScript, a critical skill for creating interactive and dynamic web applications.

Callbacks

In JavaScript, callbacks are a fundamental concept, particularly in dealing with asynchronous operations. A callback is a function passed into another function as an argument to be executed later. This section will cover basic usage of callbacks, callbacks with parameters, asynchronous callbacks, error handling in callbacks, and managing nested callbacks, often referred to as "callback hell."

Basic Callback Usage
A basic callback function is used to continue code execution after a specific task completes. It is a simple function that is called through another function.
Example: Basic Callback Usage

```
function greeting(name, callback) {
 console.log('Hello ' + name);
 callback();
}
greeting('Alice', function() {
 console.log('Callback executed');
});
```

- greeting function takes a name and a callback as arguments.
- The callback function is called right after printing the greeting message.

Callback with Parameters
Callbacks can also receive parameters, allowing data to be passed to them when they are executed.
Example: Callback with Parameters

```
function processUserInput(callback) {
 let name = prompt('Please enter your name.');
 callback(name);
}
processUserInput(function(name) {
 console.log('Hello ' + name);
});
```

- The processUserInput function collects user input and then calls the callback, passing the input data (name) to it.

Asynchronous Callback

Asynchronous callbacks are commonly used in JavaScript, especially for handling operations like reading files, making HTTP requests, or any operations that depend on external data sources and take time to complete.
Example: Asynchronous Callback
setTimeout(function() {
 console.log('This prints after 2 seconds');
}, 2000);

- setTimeout is a built-in JavaScript function that executes a callback function after a specified delay (2000 milliseconds in this example).

Error Handling in Callbacks

In Node.js and many libraries, it's common to handle errors in callbacks by passing the error as the first argument to the callback function.
Example: Error Handling in Callbacks
function fetchData(callback) {
 let data = null;
 let error = new Error('An error occurred');
 if (data) {
 callback(null, data);
 } else {
 callback(error);
 }
}
fetchData(function(err, data) {
 if (err) {
 console.error(err);
 } else {
 console.log(data);
 }
});

- The callback function is designed to accept two parameters: an error and the data.

- If there is an error, the error is passed as the first argument, and data is null. If no error, the first argument is null, and the data is passed as the second argument.

Nested Callbacks (Callback Hell)

Nested callbacks, or "callback hell," refer to several levels of nested callbacks, which can make code hard to read and maintain.

Example: Nested Callbacks (Callback Hell)

```
loginUser('alice@example.com', 'password123', function(err, user) {
if (err) {
console.log(err);
} else {
getUserSettings(user, function(err, settings) {
if (err) {
console.log(err);
} else {
updateUserSettings(user, newSettings, function(err, updated) {
if (err) {
console.log(err);
} else {
console.log('Updated settings:', updated);
}
});
}
});
}
});
```

- This code shows nested callbacks handling different stages of user interactions like logging in, fetching settings, and updating settings.
- Such nesting can lead to complex code structures that are hard to follow and debug, often referred to as "callback hell."

Understanding and properly managing callbacks is essential for effective JavaScript programming, especially in asynchronous operations. Reducing callback nesting through modularization or using Promises and async/await can help maintain cleaner and more manageable code.

Coding Exercises on Callbacks in JavaScript

Callbacks: Understanding and using callbacks for handling asynchronous operations. Here's a structured set of coding exercises and multiple-choice quiz questions focused on understanding and using callbacks for handling asynchronous operations in JavaScript. These exercises will help learners grasp how callbacks function, especially in the context of asynchronous tasks such as event handling, timing operations, and more.

Basic Callback Usage

Task: Write a function that takes a callback and executes it after printing a message.

Purpose: Understand the basic mechanism of passing functions as arguments and executing callbacks.

JavaScript Code:
```
function runCallback(callback) {
 console.log("Before executing the callback.");
 callback();
 console.log("After executing the callback.");
}
runCallback(() => {
 console.log("This is a callback function being executed.");
});
```

Explanation:
This exercise demonstrates how a callback function is passed to another function (runCallback) and gets executed within that function. It helps in understanding the control flow with callbacks, showing how code executes before, during, and after the callback.

Callback with Parameters

Task: Implement a function that takes a number and a callback, and calls the callback with the square of the number.
Purpose: Practice using callbacks with parameters to process data.
JavaScript Code:

```javascript
function processNumber(number, callback) {
 let result = number * number;
 callback(result);
}
processNumber(4, result => {
 console.log("The square of the number is:", result);
});
```

Explanation:
This function (processNumber) calculates the square of a number and passes the result to a callback, which then logs it. This showcases how callbacks can be used to handle the outcome of asynchronous operations.

Asynchronous Callback

Task: Use setTimeout with a callback to simulate an asynchronous operation that logs a message after a delay.
Purpose: Demonstrate the asynchronous nature of callbacks in JavaScript.
JavaScript Code:

```javascript
console.log("Start of script");
setTimeout(() => {
 console.log("This runs after a 2-second delay");
}, 2000);
console.log("End of script");
```

Explanation:

setTimeout is used to schedule a callback function to run after a delay of 2000 milliseconds. This shows how JavaScript handles asynchronous execution without blocking other operations.

Error Handling in Callbacks

Task: Write a function that simulates retrieving data from a server, handles errors, and success scenarios using a callback.
Purpose: Understand error handling in asynchronous callback patterns.
JavaScript Code:

```javascript
function fetchData(callback) {
let error = false; // Change this to true to simulate an error
setTimeout(() => {
if (error) {
callback('An error occurred!', null);
} else {
callback(null, { data: "Here is some fake data" });
}
}, 1000);
}
fetchData((err, data) => {
if (err) {
console.log(err);
} else {
console.log(data);
}
});
```

Explanation:
The fetchData function uses setTimeout to simulate a data fetch operation and invokes the callback with an error object and data, depending on the situation. This is a typical pattern in Node.js for handling asynchronous errors and responses.

Nested Callbacks (Callback Hell)

Task: Chain multiple asynchronous operations using callbacks, demonstrating the concept of "callback hell."

Purpose: Experience the complexity of managing multiple nested callbacks.

JavaScript Code:

```javascript
function firstTask(callback) {
 setTimeout(() => {
 console.log("First task done");
 callback();
 }, 1000);
}
function secondTask(callback) {
 setTimeout(() => {
 console.log("Second task done");
 callback();
 }, 1000);
}
function thirdTask(callback) {
 setTimeout(() => {
 console.log("Third task done");
 callback();
 }, 1000);
}
firstTask(() => {
 secondTask(() => {
 thirdTask(() => {
 console.log("All tasks completed.");
 });
 });
});
```

Explanation:

This example illustrates nested callbacks, often referred to as "callback hell," where each task starts only after the previous one has completed. It shows how readability and manageability can become challenging with multiple nested callbacks.

Multiple Choice Quiz Questions

What is a callback function in JavaScript?
A) A function that calls back the JavaScript engine to execute a task.
B) Any function that is passed as an argument to another function and is invoked after a certain event or condition.
C) A special function type that can only be used with arrays.
D) A function that can return multiple values.
Correct Answer: B) Any function that is passed as an argument to another function and is invoked after a certain event or condition.
Explanation: Callbacks are functions that are passed as arguments to other functions and are executed after certain conditions or operations complete.

Which scenario best represents a typical use of callbacks?
A) Defining functions that must execute in a particular sequence.
B) Waiting for a user to exit the page before executing the function.
C) Performing an operation after receiving data from a server.
D) Calculating mathematical operations synchronously.
Correct Answer: C) Performing an operation after receiving data from a server.
Explanation: Callbacks are often used in asynchronous operations, such as retrieving data from a server, where the callback executes once the data is available.

What issue is commonly associated with excessive use of nested callbacks?
A) Memory leaks
B) Callback hell
C) Data type errors
D) Scope creep
Correct Answer: B) Callback hell

Explanation: "Callback hell" refers to complex, nested callbacks that are difficult to read and maintain, often occurring in deeply nested asynchronous code.

How can you handle errors in a callback pattern?
A) By throwing an exception inside the callback
B) By passing the error as the first argument to the callback
C) By calling a global error handling function
D) Errors cannot be handled in callbacks
Correct Answer: B) By passing the error as the first argument to the callback
Explanation: In the callback pattern, especially in Node.js, it's conventional to handle errors by passing them as the first argument to the callback function, allowing the caller to handle the error appropriately.

What does the setTimeout function demonstrate about JavaScript callbacks?
A) Synchronous blocking behavior
B) Dependency on external libraries
C) Asynchronous non-blocking behavior
D) Incompatibility with modern JavaScript development
Correct Answer: C) Asynchronous non-blocking behavior
Explanation: setTimeout is used to illustrate how JavaScript handles asynchronous execution, allowing delays without blocking other operations, typically managed through callbacks.

These exercises and questions provide foundational and practical knowledge on using callbacks effectively in JavaScript, essential for handling asynchronous programming patterns.

Promises

Promises are a powerful tool in JavaScript for handling asynchronous operations. They represent a value that may be available now, or in the future, or never. Here, I'll explain the concepts related to promises, including creating promises, handling promise rejection, chaining promises, using Promise.all for concurrent promises, and creating and handling a failing promise in a list.

Creating a Simple Promise

Promises are objects representing the eventual completion or failure of an asynchronous operation. They are created using the Promise constructor, which takes a function called the executor.

Example: Creating a Simple Promise

```
const myPromise = new Promise((resolve, reject) => {
setTimeout(() => {
resolve('Promise resolved!');
}, 2000);
});
myPromise.then((result) => {
console.log(result); // Logs: Promise resolved!
});
```

- In this example, myPromise is a promise object that resolves after 2 seconds with the value 'Promise resolved!'.
- The then method is used to register callbacks to be called when the promise is resolved successfully.

Handling Promise Rejection

Promises can also be rejected to indicate failure. This is done by calling the reject function inside the executor function.

Example: Handling Promise Rejection

```
const myPromise = new Promise((resolve, reject) => {
setTimeout(() => {
reject(new Error('Promise rejected!'));
}, 2000);
});
```

```
myPromise.catch((error) => {
console.error(error.message); // Logs: Promise rejected!
});
```

- In this example, myPromise is a promise object that rejects after 2 seconds with an error message.
- The catch method is used to handle the rejected promise and log the error message.

Chaining Promises

Promises can be chained together using the then method, allowing for sequential execution of asynchronous operations.
Example: Chaining Promises

```
const fetchData = () => {
return new Promise((resolve) => {
setTimeout(() => {
resolve('Data fetched!');
}, 2000);
});
};
fetchData()
.then((result) => {
console.log(result); // Logs: Data fetched!
return 'Data processed!';
})
.then((result) => {
console.log(result); // Logs: Data processed!
});
```

- In this example, fetchData returns a promise that resolves after 2 seconds with the message 'Data fetched!'.
- The then method is used to chain another asynchronous operation that processes the fetched data.

Promise.all for Concurrent Promises

The Promise.all method takes an array of promises and returns a single promise that resolves when all of the promises in the array have resolved, or rejects if any of the promises reject.
Example: Promise.all for Concurrent Promises

```
const promise1 = Promise.resolve('Promise 1 resolved!');
const promise2 = new Promise((resolve) => {
setTimeout(() => {
resolve('Promise 2 resolved after 3 seconds!');
```

```
}, 3000);
});
Promise.all([promise1, promise2])
.then((results) => {
console.log(results); // Logs: ['Promise 1 resolved!', 'Promise 2
resolved after 3 seconds!']
});
```

- In this example, Promise.all is used to wait for both
  promise1 and promise2 to resolve.
- The then method is used to access the array of resolved
  values when all promises have resolved.

Creating and Handling a Failing Promise in a List

When using Promise.all with an array of promises, if any
promise in the array rejects, the entire Promise.all operation
rejects immediately.

Example: Creating and Handling a Failing Promise in a List

```
const promise1 = Promise.resolve('Promise 1 resolved!');
const promise2 = Promise.reject(new Error('Promise 2
rejected!'));
Promise.all([promise1, promise2])
.then((results) => {
console.log(results); // This line is not executed
})
.catch((error) => {
console.error(error.message); // Logs: Promise 2 rejected!
});
```

- In this example, promise2 is rejected immediately,
  causing the entire Promise.all operation to reject.
- The catch method is used to handle the rejection of the
  entire Promise.all operation.

Understanding promises and their usage is crucial for writing
clean and efficient asynchronous JavaScript code. Promises
provide a more readable and manageable way to handle
asynchronous operations compared to traditional callback-
based approaches.

Coding Exercises on Promises in JavaScript

Promises: Creating and using promises for cleaner asynchronous code. Here's a comprehensive set of coding exercises and multiple-choice quiz questions focused on understanding and using promises in JavaScript. These exercises will guide learners through creating, using, and managing promises for more effective asynchronous code handling.

Creating a Simple Promise

Task: Create a promise that resolves with the string "Hello, Promise!" after a 2-second delay.

Purpose: Learn how to create and resolve a basic promise.

JavaScript Code:

```javascript
let helloPromise = new Promise((resolve, reject) => {
setTimeout(() => {
resolve("Hello, Promise!");
}, 2000);
});
helloPromise.then(message => {
console.log(message); // Outputs "Hello, Promise!" after 2
seconds
});
```

Explanation:

This exercise introduces the construction of a promise using the Promise constructor, which takes an executor function with resolve and reject parameters. The setTimeout function simulates asynchronous operations, resolving the promise after a delay, which is then handled by .then().

Handling Promise Rejection

Task: Create a promise that rejects with an error message and use .catch() to handle the rejection.

Purpose: Practice handling errors in promises.

JavaScript Code:

```javascript
let errorPromise = new Promise((resolve, reject) => {
 setTimeout(() => {
 reject(new Error("Something went wrong!"));
 }, 1000);
});
errorPromise
 .then(result => {
 console.log(result);
 })
 .catch(error => {
 console.error(error.message); // Outputs "Something went
wrong!" after 1 second
 });
```

Explanation:

This code snippet demonstrates how to create a promise that intentionally rejects and how to handle such rejections using .catch(). It shows effective error management within asynchronous operations.

Chaining Promises

Task: Chain multiple promises to perform sequential asynchronous operations, logging the result of each step.

Purpose: Understand how to chain promises for sequential operations.

JavaScript Code:

```javascript
new Promise(resolve => resolve(1))
 .then(result => {
 console.log(result); // Outputs 1
 return result * 2;
```

```
})
.then(result => {
console.log(result); // Outputs 2
return result * 2;
})
.then(result => {
console.log(result); // Outputs 4
return result * 2;
});
```

Explanation:

This example shows how to chain .then() methods to process data sequentially. Each .then() handles the result of the previous promise and can modify the data before passing it to the next .then().

Promise.all for Concurrent Promises

Task: Use Promise.all to handle multiple promises running concurrently and log their results.

Purpose: Explore handling multiple asynchronous operations that run concurrently.

JavaScript Code:
```
let promise1 = Promise.resolve(3);
let promise2 = 42;
let promise3 = new Promise((resolve, reject) => {
setTimeout(resolve, 100, 'foo');
});
Promise.all([promise1, promise2, promise3]).then(values => {
console.log(values); // Outputs [3, 42, "foo"]
});
```

Explanation:

Promise.all takes an iterable of promises and returns a single Promise that resolves when all of the input promises have resolved. This is used to handle situations where multiple tasks need to be completed before proceeding.

Creating and Handling a Failing Promise in a List

Task: Create an array of promises where one rejects and use Promise.allSettled to handle each promise's outcome.

Purpose: Manage multiple promises and handle both success and failure cases.

JavaScript Code:

```
let promises = [
 Promise.resolve(10),
 Promise.reject(new Error("Failure")),
 Promise.resolve(30)
];
Promise.allSettled(promises).then(results => {
 results.forEach((result, index) => {
 console.log(`Promise ${index + 1}:`, result.status);
 });
});
```

Explanation:

Promise.allSettled returns a promise that resolves after all the given promises have either resolved or rejected, with an array of objects reflecting the outcome of each promise. It is useful for cases where you need to know the outcome of each promise regardless of whether they succeeded or failed.

Multiple Choice Quiz Questions

What does a JavaScript promise represent?

A) An array of functions that might not execute in order.

B) A single future value that may not yet be available.

C) A looping mechanism for asynchronous operations.

D) A synchronous callback function.

Correct Answer: B) A single future value that may not yet be available.

Explanation: A promise in JavaScript represents a value that may not yet be available but will be resolved at some point in the future.

Which method is used to execute code after a promise is resolved or rejected?
A) Promise.then()
B) Promise.catch()
C) Promise.finally()
D) Promise.resolve()
Correct Answer: C) Promise.finally()
Explanation: The finally() method returns a promise. When the promise is settled, i.e., either fulfilled or rejected, the specified callback function is executed. This provides a way for code to be run whether the promise was fulfilled successfully or rejected.

How can you handle errors in a chain of promises?
A) Using a loop to catch errors in each promise.
B) Using the .error() method at the end of the chain.
C) Using a single .catch() method at the end of the chain.
D) Errors in promises cannot be caught.
Correct Answer: C) Using a single .catch() method at the end of the chain.
Explanation: Placing a .catch() at the end of a promise chain ensures that any error thrown in the chain can be caught and handled appropriately.

What does Promise.all do?
A) It resolves all promises in the array regardless of whether some are rejected.
B) It rejects as soon as one of the promises in the array rejects.
C) It only resolves if all promises are rejected.
D) It increases the speed of promise resolution.
Correct Answer: B) It rejects as soon as one of the promises in the array rejects.

Explanation: Promise.all is an all-or-nothing method that resolves only if all promises in the iterable resolve. It rejects immediately if any of the promises reject.

What advantage does Promise.allSettled have over Promise.all?
A) It resolves immediately after the first promise settles.
B) It only returns successful results.
C) It waits for all promises to settle, regardless of whether they resolve or reject.
D) It rejects all promises if at least one fails.
Correct Answer: C) It waits for all promises to settle, regardless of whether they resolve or reject.
Explanation: Promise.allSettled returns a promise that resolves after all the given promises have either resolved or rejected, with an array of objects that each describe the outcome of each promise.

These exercises and questions provide a solid foundation in understanding and using promises to handle asynchronous operations in JavaScript, crucial for modern web application development.

Async/Await:

Async/await is a modern JavaScript feature that allows for writing asynchronous code in a synchronous manner, making it easier to read and maintain. Below, I'll explain the concepts related to async/await, including basic usage, error handling, chaining async operations, using async/await with array methods, and making external API calls.

Basic Async/Await Usage
The async keyword is used to define a function as asynchronous, and the await keyword is used to wait for a promise to resolve before proceeding with code execution.
Example: Basic Async/Await Usage

```
async function fetchData() {
  const response = await fetch('https://api.example.com/data');
  const data = await response.json();
  return data;
}
fetchData().then((data) => {
  console.log(data);
});
```

- In this example, fetchData is an asynchronous function that fetches data from an API.
- The await keyword is used to wait for the promise returned by fetch to resolve, and then for the JSON parsing to complete.
- The function returns the parsed data.

Async/Await with Error Handling
Async/await simplifies error handling by allowing the use of try/catch blocks around asynchronous code.
Example: Async/Await with Error Handling

```
async function fetchData() {
  try {
  const response = await fetch('https://api.example.com/data');
  const data = await response.json();
  return data;
  } catch (error) {
  console.error('Error fetching data:', error);
  throw error;
```

```
}
}
fetchData().catch((error) => {
// Handle error
});
```

- In this example, a try/catch block is used to catch any errors that occur during the asynchronous operations inside the fetchData function.
- If an error occurs, it is logged, and then rethrown to be caught by the caller.

Chaining Async Operations

Async/await allows for easy chaining of multiple asynchronous operations in a synchronous-looking manner.

Example: Chaining Async Operations

```
async function fetchAndProcessData() {
const data = await fetchData();
const processedData = await processData(data);
return processedData;
}
fetchAndProcessData().then((result) => {
console.log(result);
});
```

- In this example, fetchAndProcessData asynchronously fetches data and then processes it.
- The await keyword ensures that each operation completes before proceeding to the next one.

Using Async/Await with Array Methods

Async/await can be used with array methods like map, filter, and reduce to perform asynchronous operations on array elements.

Example: Using Async/Await with Array Methods

```
async function processArray(array) {
const processedArray = await Promise.all(array.map(async
(item) => {
const processedItem = await processItem(item);
return processedItem;
}));
return processedArray;
}
```

```
processArray(myArray).then((result) => {
 console.log(result);
});
```

- In this example, processArray asynchronously processes each item in the input array using the map method and the processItem function.
- Promise.all is used to wait for all promises to resolve before returning the result.

Async/Await with External API Calls

Async/await is commonly used with external API calls to simplify asynchronous code and improve readability.
Example: Async/Await with External API Calls

```
async function fetchDataFromAPI() {
 const response = await fetch('https://api.example.com/data');
 const data = await response.json();
 return data;
}
fetchDataFromAPI().then((data) => {
 console.log(data);
});
```

- In this example, fetchDataFromAPI asynchronously fetches data from an external API using the fetch function.
- The await keyword is used to wait for the response to resolve before parsing it as JSON.

Async/await simplifies asynchronous programming in JavaScript, making it easier to write and understand code that deals with asynchronous operations such as fetching data from APIs, reading files, or waiting for timeouts. It improves code readability and maintainability by eliminating callback nesting and reducing error handling boilerplate.

Coding Exercises on Async/Await in JavaScript

Async/Await: Modern syntax for handling asynchronous operations, making code easier to read and maintain.
Here's a set of coding exercises and multiple-choice quiz questions focusing on async/await, a modern JavaScript syntax for handling asynchronous operations. These exercises will help learners understand how async/await simplifies writing asynchronous code by making it more readable and easier to maintain.

Basic Async/Await Usage

Task: Create an async function that uses setTimeout to simulate a delay, then logs a message.
Purpose: Understand the basic structure of an async function and how to use await with setTimeout.
JavaScript Code:

```
function delay(ms) {
 return new Promise(resolve => setTimeout(resolve, ms));
}
async function performTask() {
 console.log("Task started");
 await delay(2000); // Wait for 2 seconds
 console.log("Task completed after a delay");
}
performTask();
```

Explanation:
This exercise introduces the async function performTask, which waits for a promise returned by the delay function to resolve before continuing. This shows how await can pause function execution in a way that's non-blocking to the rest of the code execution.

122

Async/Await with Error Handling

Task: Use try, catch, and finally within an async function to handle potential errors and ensure some code runs after completion.

Purpose: Practice error handling within async/await syntax.

JavaScript Code:

```javascript
async function fetchData(url) {
try {
const response = await fetch(url);
const data = await response.json();
console.log("Data retrieved:", data);
} catch (error) {
console.error("An error occurred:", error);
} finally {
console.log("Fetch attempt finished.");
}
}
fetchData("https://api.example.com/data");
```

Explanation:

This script attempts to fetch data from a specified URL. If fetching or parsing the data fails, the error is caught and logged. The finally block ensures that a message is logged regardless of the outcome, demonstrating comprehensive error handling.

Chaining Async Operations

Task: Write an async function that performs a series of dependent asynchronous operations sequentially.

Purpose: Learn how to chain asynchronous operations that depend on the output of previous operations.

JavaScript Code:

```javascript
// Simulated asynchronous functions
function doFirstThing() {
    return new Promise((resolve) => {
        setTimeout(() => {
```

```javascript
      resolve('First result');
    }, 1000);
  });
}
function doSecondThing(data) {
  return new Promise((resolve) => {
    setTimeout(() => {
      resolve(`Second result based on ${data}`);
    }, 1000);
  });
}
function doThirdThing(data) {
  return new Promise((resolve) => {
    setTimeout(() => {
      resolve(`Third result based on ${data}`);
    }, 1000);
  });
}
// Async function chaining
async function chainOperations() {
  try {
    const firstResult = await doFirstThing();
    const secondResult = await doSecondThing(firstResult);
    const finalResult = await doThirdThing(secondResult);
    console.log("Final result:", finalResult);
  } catch (error) {
    console.error("An error occurred:", error);
  }
}

chainOperations();
```

Explanation:

Each step in chainOperations waits for the previous operation to complete before starting the next. This serial execution pattern shows how async/await can simplify handling dependencies in asynchronous workflows.

Using Async/Await with Array Methods

Task: Use async/await with Array.prototype.map() to perform asynchronous operations on array items.
Purpose: Demonstrate handling arrays of promises with async/await.
JavaScript Code:

```
async function processArray(array) {
 const promises = array.map(async item => {
 await delay(1000); // Simulate a delay
 return item * 2;
 });
 const results = await Promise.all(promises);
 console.log("Processed results:", results);
}
processArray([1, 2, 3, 4]);
```

Explanation:
This code processes each item in an array by doubling it after a delay. Promise.all is used to wait for all mapped promises to resolve, showcasing how to combine async/await with array processing.

Async/Await with External API Calls

Task: Create an async function to retrieve data from an external API and log it.
Purpose: Apply async/await for real-world external API interaction.
JavaScript Code:

```
async function getUser(userId) {
```

```
 const response = await
fetch(`https://jsonplaceholder.typicode.com/users/${userId}`
);
 const user = await response.json();
 console.log("User data:", user);
}
getUser(1);
```

Explanation:

The getUser function makes an HTTP request to a public API and processes the JSON response. This demonstrates the practical application of async/await in dealing with real-world asynchronous operations like HTTP requests.

Multiple Choice Quiz Questions

What is the primary benefit of using async/await in JavaScript?

A) It automatically handles all errors.

B) It makes asynchronous code easier to write and read.

C) It speeds up the execution of asynchronous code.

D) It replaces all promises with synchronous functions.

Correct Answer: B) It makes asynchronous code easier to write and read.

Explanation: Async/await simplifies the syntax and management of asynchronous operations, making the code more understandable compared to traditional promise syntax.

Which statement is true about async functions?

A) They always return a promise.

B) They execute synchronously.

C) They can only use try/catch for error handling.

D) They prevent JavaScript from executing other code until they complete.

Correct Answer: A) They always return a promise.

Explanation: async functions return a promise implicitly, and the return value of the async function is resolved as the value of the promise.

How can you correctly handle errors in an async function?
A) Using a for loop.
B) Using a while loop.
C) Using try/catch blocks.
D) Using if/else statements.
Correct Answer: C) Using try/catch blocks.
Explanation: try/catch is effective for handling errors in async functions, allowing for the catching of exceptions thrown during asynchronous operations.

What does the await keyword do in an async function?
A) Pauses the function execution until the promise settles.
B) Immediately runs a callback function.
C) Returns a new promise.
D) Sends a request to the server.
Correct Answer: A) Pauses the function execution until the promise settles.
Explanation: await pauses the async function and waits for the Promise to resolve or reject, and then resumes the async function's execution and returns the resolved value.

Can await be used outside of an async function?
A) Yes, in any JavaScript function.
B) Yes, but only inside functions declared with async.
C) No, it causes a syntax error if used outside of an async function.
D) No, unless the script is module type.
Correct Answer: C) No, it causes a syntax error if used outside of an async function.
Explanation: The await keyword is only valid inside async functions and using it outside of such functions will result in a syntax error.

These exercises and questions provide a thorough understanding of async/await in JavaScript, showing its effectiveness in making asynchronous code cleaner and more manageable.

Working with APIs

Working with APIs in JavaScript involves interacting with remote servers to fetch or send data. The fetch API is a modern way to make network requests, providing a simpler and more powerful interface compared to traditional methods like XMLHttpRequest. Below, I'll explain the concepts related to working with APIs using fetch, including making basic fetch requests, fetching and displaying data, handling network errors, making POST requests, and using async/await with fetch.

Basic Fetch Request

The fetch function is used to make HTTP requests to remote servers and returns a promise that resolves to the Response object representing the response to the request.
Example: Basic Fetch Request

```
fetch('https://api.example.com/data')
 .then(response => response.json())
 .then(data => console.log(data))
 .catch(error => console.error('Error fetching data:', error));
```

- In this example, fetch is used to make a GET request to the specified URL (https://api.example.com/data).
- The then method is used to parse the JSON response using the json method of the Response object.
- Subsequent then methods handle the parsed data, and a catch method handles any errors that occur during the fetch operation.

Fetching and Displaying Data

Once data is fetched from an API, it can be displayed in the user interface or processed further as needed.
Example: Fetching and Displaying Data

```
fetch('https://api.example.com/data')
 .then(response => response.json())
 .then(data => {
// Display data in the UI
document.getElementById('result').textContent = data;
})
 .catch(error => console.error('Error fetching data:', error));
```

- In this example, the fetched data is displayed in the UI by setting the text content of an element with the ID result to the fetched data.

Handling Network Errors

When working with APIs, it's essential to handle network errors gracefully to provide a good user experience.
Example: Handling Network Errors

```
fetch('https://api.example.com/data')
.then(response => {
if (!response.ok) {
throw new Error('Network response was not ok');
}
return response.json();
})
.then(data => console.log(data))
.catch(error => console.error('Error fetching data:', error));
```

- In this example, the ok property of the Response object is checked to determine if the request was successful.
- If the response is not okay, an error is thrown and caught by the catch method.

POST Request Using Fetch

Fetch can also be used to make POST requests by providing additional options in the fetch call.
Example: POST Request Using Fetch

```
fetch('https://api.example.com/submit', {
method: 'POST',
headers: {
'Content-Type': 'application/json',
},
body: JSON.stringify({ key: 'value' }),
})
.then(response => response.json())
.then(data => console.log(data))
.catch(error => console.error('Error:', error));
```

- In this example, the method option is set to 'POST', and the body option is used to send data to the server in JSON format.

Using Async/Await with Fetch

Async/await can simplify the code for making fetch requests, especially when chaining multiple requests or handling complex data.

Example: Using Async/Await with Fetch

```
async function fetchData() {
try {
const response = await fetch('https://api.example.com/data');
const data = await response.json();
console.log(data);
} catch (error) {
console.error('Error fetching data:', error);
}
}
fetchData();
```

- In this example, an async function fetchData is defined to make a fetch request and parse the JSON response using await.
- Any errors that occur during the fetch operation are caught and logged in the catch block.

Working with APIs using fetch allows for seamless integration of external data into web applications. By understanding how to use fetch effectively, you can build dynamic and interactive applications that fetch, display, and manipulate data from various sources on the internet.

Coding Exercises on Fetching Data with fetch

Working with APIs: Fetching data from external APIs using fetch. Here's a collection of coding exercises and multiple-choice quiz questions focused on working with APIs in JavaScript using the fetch method. These exercises will help learners understand how to fetch data from external APIs, process JSON responses, and handle potential errors.

Basic Fetch Request

Task: Fetch data from a JSON placeholder API and log the JSON response.

Purpose: Learn to perform GET requests with fetch and handle JSON data.

JavaScript Code:

```
fetch('https://jsonplaceholder.typicode.com/posts/1')
 .then(response => response.json())
 .then(json => console.log(json))
 .catch(error => console.error('Error fetching data:', error));
```

Explanation:

This exercise demonstrates the basic usage of the fetch API to make a GET request to a JSON placeholder service. It shows how to chain .then() to handle the promise returned by fetch, convert the response to JSON, and then process it. Error handling is shown using .catch().

Fetching and Displaying Data

Task: Fetch a list of users from an API and display their names in an HTML list.

Purpose: Combine data fetching with DOM manipulation to display data.

HTML + JavaScript Code:

```
<ul id="userList"></ul>
<script>
fetch('https://jsonplaceholder.typicode.com/users')
 .then(response => response.json())
 .then(users => {
 const userList = document.getElementById('userList');
 users.forEach(user => {
 const li = document.createElement('li');
 li.textContent = user.name;
 userList.appendChild(li);
 });
```

```
})
.catch(error => console.error('Error loading user data:', error));
</script>
```

Explanation:

This script fetches data about users and processes it by iterating over the returned array. It dynamically creates list items for each user and appends them to an unordered list in the DOM. This demonstrates how to handle asynchronous data and update the DOM accordingly.

Handling Network Errors

Task: Fetch data from an API and handle network errors gracefully.

Purpose: Implement error handling to manage common issues like network failures.

JavaScript Code:

```
fetch('https://jsonplaceholder.typicode.com/posts/2')
.then(response => {
if (!response.ok) {
throw new Error('Network response was not ok ' +
response.statusText);
}
return response.json();
})
.then(json => console.log(json))
.catch(error => console.error('Failed to fetch:', error));
```

Explanation:

This code checks the response status using response.ok. If there is a problem (e.g., response status is not in the 200-299 range), it throws an error that is then caught by the .catch() block, thus providing robust error handling.

POST Request Using Fetch

Task: Send data to an API using a POST request with fetch.
Purpose: Learn to use fetch for sending data to a server.
JavaScript Code:

```
fetch('https://jsonplaceholder.typicode.com/posts', {
 method: 'POST',
 headers: {
 'Content-Type': 'application/json'
 },
 body: JSON.stringify({
 title: 'foo',
 body: 'bar',
 userId: 1
 })
})
.then(response => response.json())
.then(json => console.log('Post created:', json))
.catch(error => console.error('Error posting data:', error));
```

Explanation:
This exercise shows how to make a POST request using fetch by specifying the method, headers, and body. It uses JSON.stringify to convert a JavaScript object into a JSON string, which is then sent in the request body.

Using Async/Await with Fetch

Task: Rewrite a fetch request using async/await for cleaner syntax.
Purpose: Practice using modern JavaScript features to simplify asynchronous code.
JavaScript Code:

```
async function fetchPost() {
 try {
 const response = await
fetch('https://jsonplaceholder.typicode.com/posts/3');
```

```
if (!response.ok) {
throw new Error('Failed to fetch: ' + response.statusText);
}
const post = await response.json();
console.log(post);
} catch (error) {
console.error(error);
}
}
fetchPost();
```

Explanation:

This function demonstrates how to use async/await with fetch for making asynchronous HTTP requests more readable and easier to manage. It includes error handling directly within the async function using try/catch.

Multiple Choice Quiz Questions

What does the fetch function return?

A) A JSON object

B) An immediately resolved promise

C) A promise that resolves with the response to the request

D) The actual data requested

Correct Answer: C) A promise that resolves with the response to the request

Explanation: fetch returns a promise that resolves to the Response object representing the response to the request, not the actual data.

Which HTTP method is used by default when using fetch?

A) POST

B) GET

C) DELETE

D) PUT

Correct Answer: B) GET

Explanation: When no method is specified, fetch uses the GET method by default to retrieve data from the specified resource.

How can you send data as JSON using fetch?
A) By adding a query string to the URL
B) By using FormData object as the body
C) By setting the body to a JSON string and setting Content-Type header to application/json
D) JSON cannot be sent using fetch

Correct Answer: C) By setting the body to a JSON string and setting Content-Type header to application/json

Explanation: To send JSON data using fetch, you must stringify the data and set the Content-Type header to application/json.

What is the purpose of the .catch() method in a fetch chain?
A) To parse JSON from the response
B) To catch any errors that occur during the fetch operation
C) To resend the request if it fails
D) To increase the request timeout

Correct Answer: B) To catch any errors that occur during the fetch operation

Explanation: .catch() is used in promise chains to handle any errors that may occur during the fetch operation or processing of the response.

Which method on the Response object is used to extract JSON from the fetch response?
A) .json()
B) .text()
C) .data()
D) .blob()

Correct Answer: A) .json()

Explanation: The .json() method on the Response object is used to read the response stream and parse it as JSON.

These exercises and questions offer a foundational understanding of how to fetch data from APIs using fetch in JavaScript, crucial for interacting with external data sources effectively.

HTTP Methods

HTTP methods are verbs that describe the action to be performed on a resource identified by a URL. They are fundamental to how clients and servers communicate over the HTTP protocol. Below, I'll explain the concepts related to HTTP methods, including using GET to fetch data, creating data with POST, updating data with PUT, performing partial updates with PATCH, and deleting data with DELETE.

Using GET to Fetch Data
The GET method is used to request data from a specified resource.
Example: Using GET to Fetch Data

```
fetch('https://api.example.com/data', {
 method: 'GET'
})
.then(response => response.json())
.then(data => console.log(data))
.catch(error => console.error('Error fetching data:', error));
```

- In this example, the fetch function is used to make a GET request to fetch data from the specified URL (https://api.example.com/data).
- The method option is set to 'GET' to indicate that a GET request should be made.

Creating Data with POST
The POST method is used to submit data to be processed to a specified resource.
Example: Creating Data with POST

```
fetch('https://api.example.com/data', {
 method: 'POST',
 headers: {
 'Content-Type': 'application/json'
 },
 body: JSON.stringify({ key: 'value' })
})
.then(response => response.json())
.then(data => console.log(data))
.catch(error => console.error('Error creating data:', error));
```

- In this example, the fetch function is used to make a POST request to send data to the specified URL (https://api.example.com/data).
- The method option is set to 'POST', and the data to be sent is specified in the body option as JSON format using JSON.stringify.

Updating Data with PUT

The PUT method is used to update a resource or create a new resource if it does not exist.

Example: Updating Data with PUT

```
fetch('https://api.example.com/data/123', {
method: 'PUT',
headers: {
'Content-Type': 'application/json'
},
body: JSON.stringify({ key: 'new value' })
})
.then(response => response.json())
.then(data => console.log(data))
.catch(error => console.error('Error updating data:', error));
```

- In this example, the fetch function is used to make a PUT request to update the resource identified by the URL (https://api.example.com/data/123).
- The method option is set to 'PUT', and the updated data is specified in the body option as JSON format using JSON.stringify.

Partial Update with PATCH

The PATCH method is used to apply partial modifications to a resource.

Example: Partial Update with PATCH

```
fetch('https://api.example.com/data/123', {
method: 'PATCH',
headers: {
'Content-Type': 'application/json'
},
body: JSON.stringify({ key: 'partial value' })
})
.then(response => response.json())
.then(data => console.log(data))
.catch(error => console.error('Error updating data:', error));
```

139

- In this example, the fetch function is used to make a PATCH request to apply partial updates to the resource identified by the URL (https://api.example.com/data/123).
- The method option is set to 'PATCH', and the partial update data is specified in the body option as JSON format using JSON.stringify.

Deleting Data with DELETE

The DELETE method is used to delete a resource identified by a specified URL.

Example: Deleting Data with DELETE

```
fetch('https://api.example.com/data/123', {
 method: 'DELETE'
})
.then(response => {
 if (response.ok) {
 console.log('Data deleted successfully');
 } else {
 console.error('Failed to delete data');
 }
})
.catch(error => console.error('Error deleting data:', error));
```

- In this example, the fetch function is used to make a DELETE request to delete the resource identified by the URL (https://api.example.com/data/123).
- The method option is set to 'DELETE'.
- The response.ok property is checked to determine if the request was successful.

Understanding HTTP methods is essential for building web applications that interact with servers to perform various actions such as fetching, creating, updating, and deleting data. By using the appropriate HTTP methods, you can ensure that your application communicates effectively with the server and follows RESTful principles for building scalable and maintainable APIs.

Coding Exercises on HTTP Methods

HTTP Methods: Understanding GET, POST, PUT, DELETE methods. Here's a set of coding exercises and multiple-choice quiz questions focused on understanding HTTP methods such as GET, POST, PUT, and DELETE in JavaScript using the fetch API. These exercises will help learners understand how to implement each HTTP method to interact with APIs effectively.

Using GET to Fetch Data

Task: Fetch and log data from a public API.
Purpose: Learn to retrieve data using the GET method.
JavaScript Code:

```
fetch('https://jsonplaceholder.typicode.com/posts/1')
 .then(response => response.json())
 .then(data => console.log(data))
 .catch(error => console.error('Failed to fetch:', error));
```

Explanation:
This exercise demonstrates how to use the GET method with fetch to request data from an API. The .then() method processes the response to JSON, which is then logged to the console. Error handling is included to catch any issues during the fetch operation.

Creating Data with POST

Task: Send data to create a new resource at an API endpoint.
Purpose: Practice using the POST method to submit data.
JavaScript Code:

```
fetch('https://jsonplaceholder.typicode.com/posts', {
 method: 'POST',
 headers: {
 'Content-Type': 'application/json'
```

```
},
body: JSON.stringify({
title: 'foo',
body: 'bar',
userId: 1
})
})
.then(response => response.json())
.then(data => console.log('Created:', data))
.catch(error => console.error('Error posting data:', error));
```

Explanation:

This code uses the POST method to send new data to the server. The headers specify that the request body format is JSON. The response is then processed and logged, showcasing how to create new data entries on the server.

Updating Data with PUT

Task: Update existing data on a server.

Purpose: Understand how to use the PUT method to update a resource completely.

JavaScript Code:

```
fetch('https://jsonplaceholder.typicode.com/posts/1', {
method: 'PUT',
headers: {
'Content-Type': 'application/json'
},
body: JSON.stringify({
id: 1,
title: 'Updated Title',
body: 'Updated body',
userId: 1
})
})
.then(response => response.json())
```

.then(data => console.log('Updated:', data))
.catch(error => console.error('Error updating data:', error));
Explanation:
The PUT method is used to update an existing entry entirely. This example sends a complete new object that replaces the old one at the specified ID, demonstrating the full replacement nature of PUT.

Partial Update with PATCH

Task: Partially update a resource using PATCH.
Purpose: Show how to make partial updates with PATCH, differentiating from PUT.
JavaScript Code:

```
fetch('https://jsonplaceholder.typicode.com/posts/1', {
  method: 'PATCH',
  headers: {
    'Content-Type': 'application/json'
  },
  body: JSON.stringify({
    title: 'Patched Title'
  })
})
.then(response => response.json())
.then(data => console.log('Patched:', data))
.catch(error => console.error('Error patching data:', error));
```

Explanation:
PATCH is used for making partial updates to an existing resource, where only specific fields are sent to be updated. This example updates only the title of the post without altering other fields.

Deleting Data with DELETE

Task: Delete a resource from the server.

Purpose: Learn to remove data using the DELETE method.
JavaScript Code:

```
fetch('https://jsonplaceholder.typicode.com/posts/1', {
 method: 'DELETE'
})
.then(() => console.log('Deleted successfully'))
.catch(error => console.error('Error deleting data:', error));
```

Explanation:
This example uses the DELETE method to remove a resource specified by its ID. The response does not typically contain content, but the status of the operation is logged.

Multiple Choice Quiz Questions

What HTTP method is commonly used to retrieve data from a server?
A) POST
B) GET
C) DELETE
D) PUT
Correct Answer: B) GET
Explanation: The GET method is primarily used to request data from a server and does not alter the state of the resource.

Which HTTP method should you use to create a new resource?
A) GET
B) POST
C) PATCH
D) PUT
Correct Answer: B) POST
Explanation: POST is used to send data to a server to create a new resource.

What is the main difference between PUT and PATCH methods?

A) PUT updates all parts of a resource; PATCH can update specific parts.

B) PUT is faster than PATCH.

C) PATCH creates new resources; PUT does not.

D) There is no difference; they are interchangeable.

Correct Answer: A) PUT updates all parts of a resource; PATCH can update specific parts.

Explanation: PUT is used for updating a resource completely, while PATCH is used for making partial updates to a resource.

What does the DELETE method do?

A) Retrieves data to be deleted.

B) Updates data that will be deleted.

C) Removes data from the server.

D) None of the above.

Correct Answer: C) Removes data from the server.

Explanation: DELETE is used to delete resources from the server.

When using the fetch API, what property must be set to specify the HTTP method?

A) method

B) header

C) body

D) type

Correct Answer: A) method

Explanation: When making a request with fetch, the method property of the options object is used to specify the HTTP method (e.g., GET, POST, PUT, DELETE).

These exercises and questions offer comprehensive insights into using different HTTP methods effectively in JavaScript, which is crucial for interacting with APIs.

JavaScript Modules

JavaScript modules provide a way to organize code into reusable units. They allow you to encapsulate functionality and selectively expose parts of it to other parts of your application. Below, I'll explain the concepts related to JavaScript modules, including creating and exporting a module, importing a module, default exports, and renaming imports and exports.

The type="module" attribute in a <script> tag is used to indicate that the script should be treated as an ES6 module. When a browser encounters a script tag with type="module", it knows to load the script as a module and handle its dependencies accordingly. Here's how it works:

1. Module Loading: When a browser encounters a script tag with type="module", it treats the script as an ES6 module. This means that the script is loaded asynchronously, and its dependencies are fetched and executed in parallel.

2. Isolation: Modules loaded with type="module" have their own scope. This means that variables, functions, and classes defined in one module are not accessible in other modules unless explicitly exported and imported.

3. Dependency Resolution: When a module imports other modules using import statements, the browser automatically resolves the dependencies and fetches the imported modules before executing the current module.

4. Strict Mode: Modules are automatically executed in strict mode ('use strict';). This helps catch common programming errors and promotes cleaner code.

5. CORS Policy: Modules loaded with type="module" are subject to the Cross-Origin Resource Sharing (CORS) policy. This means that they can only import modules from the same origin unless the server explicitly allows cross-origin requests.

Here's an example of how to use type="module" in a script tag:

```
<!DOCTYPE html>
<html lang="en">
<head>
```

```html
    <meta charset="UTF-8">
    <meta name="viewport" content="width=device-width,
initial-scale=1.0">
    <title>Module Example</title>
</head>
<body>
    <!-- Load a module script -->
    <script type="module" src="main.js"></script>
</body>
</html>
```

In this example, the main.js script will be treated as an ES6
module, and the browser will load it accordingly. You can then
use import and export statements in main.js to work with other
modules in your application.

Creating and Exporting a Module

To create a module in JavaScript, you can define functions,
variables, or classes within a file and use the export keyword to
export them.

Example: Creating and Exporting a Module

```javascript
// math.js
export function add(a, b) {
 return a + b;
}
export function subtract(a, b) {
 return a - b;
}
```

- In this example, a module named math is created,
  which contains two functions: add and subtract.
- The export keyword is used to export each function,
  making them accessible to other modules.

Importing a Module

To use functions, variables, or classes from a module in another
module, you can use the import keyword followed by the
module's path and the name of the exported item.

Example: Importing a Module

```javascript
// main.js
import { add, subtract } from './math.js';
console.log(add(5, 3)); // Output: 8
console.log(subtract(10, 4)); // Output: 6
```

- In this example, the add and subtract functions from the math module are imported into the main module.
- The functions can then be used just like any other function in the main module.

Default Exports

In addition to named exports, a module can have a default export, which represents the main functionality of the module.
Example: Default Export

```
// utility.js
export default function greet(name) {
 return `Hello, ${name}!`;
}
```

- In this example, the greet function is exported as the default export of the utility module.
- Default exports are imported without using braces and can be renamed during import.

Importing a Default Export

To import a default export from a module, you can use the import keyword followed by the module's path and an alias for the default export.
Example: Importing a Default Export

```
// app.js
import customGreet from './utility.js';
console.log(customGreet('Alice')); // Output: Hello, Alice!
```

- In this example, the greet function from the utility module is imported as customGreet in the app module.
- The function can then be used using the alias customGreet.

Renaming Imports and Exports

You can rename imported or exported items using the as keyword.
Example: Renaming Imports and Exports

```
// constants.js
const PI = 3.14159;
export { PI as PI_VALUE };
```

- In this example, the constant PI is exported from the constants module as PI_VALUE.

- When importing, you can use the new name PI_VALUE to refer to the exported constant.

JavaScript modules provide a clean and modular way to structure your code, making it easier to manage and maintain large applications. By exporting and importing specific parts of your code, you can create a clear separation of concerns and improve code reuse and readability.

Coding Exercises on JavaScript ES6 Modules

JavaScript Modules: Understanding ES6 modules (import/export) for better code organization. Here's a structured guide with coding exercises and multiple-choice quiz questions focused on understanding and using ES6 modules in JavaScript. These exercises will help learners grasp the concepts of importing and exporting modules, which are essential for organizing code more effectively and maintaining larger applications.

Creating and Exporting a Module

Task: Create a module that exports a function to calculate the area of a rectangle.
Purpose: Learn to define and export a module.
JavaScript Code (rectangle.js):

```javascript
// Define and export the area function
export function area(width, height) {
 return width * height;
}
```

Explanation:

This exercise shows how to create a simple function that calculates the area of a rectangle and exports it. Using export before the function declaration makes it accessible to other modules.

Importing a Module

Task: Import the area function from the rectangle module and use it in a different file.

Purpose: Practice importing functions from one module to another.

JavaScript Code (main.js):

```
// Import the area function from rectangle.js
import { area } from './rectangle.js';
// Use the imported function
console.log("Area of rectangle:", area(5, 3)); // Outputs: Area
of rectangle: 15
```

rectangle.js

```
// Define and export the area function
export function area(width, height) {
    return width * height;
}
```

Explanation:

This script demonstrates how to import a function from a module using curly braces {} and use it just like any locally defined function. This separation of concerns aids in maintaining cleaner code.

Default Exports

Task: Create a module that has a default export of a class.

Purpose: Understand the usage of default exports in modules.

JavaScript Code (User.js):

```
// Define a User class and export it as default
export default class User {
```

```
constructor(name, age) {
this.name = name;
this.age = age;
}
greet() {
return `Hello, my name is ${this.name} and I am ${this.age}
years old.`;
}
}
// main.js
import User from './User.js';
// Create a new instance of the User class
const user = new User('John', 30);
// Call the greet method
console.log(user.greet()); // Output: Hello, my name is John
and I am 30 years old.
```

Explanation:
The User class is exported as the default export of the module.
Default exports are useful when a module is intended to export
a single main functionality, such as a class or a library.

Importing a Default Export

Task: Import the default User class from its module and create
an instance.
Purpose: Learn to import a default export from a module.
JavaScript Code (app.js):
```
// Import the default export from User.js
import User from './User.js';
// Create an instance of User
const newUser = new User("John Doe", 30);
console.log(newUser.greet()); // Outputs: Hello, my name is
John Doe and I am 30 years old.
```
Explanation:

This script imports the User class (a default export) and uses it to create a User object. It showcases how default exports are imported without curly braces.

Renaming Imports and Exports

Task: Import specific functions from a module and rename them for local use.

Purpose: Learn to use aliases in import statements.

JavaScript Code (utilities.js):

```
export function add(x, y) {
  return x + y;
}
export function subtract(x, y) {
  return x - y;
}
```

JavaScript Code (calc.js):

```
// Import with renaming
import { add as addition, subtract as subtraction } from './utilities.js';
console.log("Addition result:", addition(10, 5)); // Outputs: Addition result: 15
console.log("Subtraction result:", subtraction(10, 5)); // Outputs: Subtraction result: 5
```

Explanation:

This exercise shows how to rename imports to avoid naming conflicts or to provide more context in the local scope. It's particularly useful in large projects where name clashes are possible.

Multiple Choice Quiz Questions

What is the main purpose of using export in a JavaScript module?

A) To load functions from another module
B) To share code across different files
C) To increase performance
D) To secure the code
Correct Answer: B) To share code across different files
Explanation: The export statement is used in JavaScript modules to make parts of a module available for use in other files.

Which statement correctly imports a default export from a module?
A) import { default as User } from './User.js';
B) import User from './User.js';
C) import './User.js';
D) import * as User from './User.js';
Correct Answer: B) import User from './User.js';
Explanation: The default export of a module can be imported using a simple import statement without curly braces.

When would you use named exports over default exports?
A) When you only need to export one value from a module
B) When you want to export multiple values from a module
C) When the export values do not need to be used in other files
D) When the module does not interact with other modules
Correct Answer: B) When you want to export multiple values from a module
Explanation: Named exports are ideal for exporting multiple values, allowing specific imports of only the needed parts of a module.

What is the correct way to import multiple specific functions from a module?
A) import { functionOne, functionTwo } from './module.js';
B) import * from './module.js';
C) import './module.js';
D) import functionOne, functionTwo from './module.js';

Correct Answer: A) import { functionOne, functionTwo } from './module.js';
Explanation: To import multiple specific functions or values, use the named import syntax with curly braces.

How can you handle a naming conflict when importing a function?

A) By importing the module only
B) By changing the function name in the module
C) By using an alias in the import statement
D) By not importing the conflicting function
Correct Answer: C) By using an alias in the import statement
Explanation: Aliases can be used during the import to resolve naming conflicts or provide more descriptive names locally.

These exercises and questions provide comprehensive insights into using ES6 modules effectively, enhancing code organization and maintainability in JavaScript development.

Modern JavaScript Features

Template Literals
Template literals provide a more flexible and readable way to work with strings in JavaScript. They allow embedding expressions directly within strings and support multiline strings.
Example: Template Literals
const name = 'John';
const age = 30;
const greeting = `Hello, my name is ${name} and I am ${age} years old.`;
console.log(greeting);

- In this example, the ${} syntax within backticks (`) allows embedding variables directly into the string.
- Template literals support multiline strings without needing to concatenate multiple strings or use escape characters.

Arrow Functions
Arrow functions provide a more concise syntax for defining functions, especially for simple one-liners. They also inherit the lexical scope from the surrounding code.
Example: Arrow Functions
const add = (a, b) => a + b;
const greet = name => `Hello, ${name}!`;
console.log(add(2, 3)); // Output: 5
console.log(greet('Alice')); // Output: Hello, Alice!

- Arrow functions are defined using the (parameters) => expression syntax.
- They have an implicit return if there's only one expression, which makes them concise for simple functions.

let and const
let and const are block-scoped variable declarations introduced in ES6. let allows reassignment, while const declares a constant value.
Example: let and const
let count = 0;
count = 1;
const PI = 3.14;

155

- let allows variables to be reassigned after declaration, while const variables cannot be reassigned after initialization.
- Both let and const are block-scoped, meaning they are only accessible within the block in which they are defined.

Object Destructuring

Object destructuring provides a concise syntax for extracting values from objects and assigning them to variables.
Example: Object Destructuring

```
const person = {
 firstName: 'John',
 lastName: 'Doe',
 age: 30
};
const { firstName, lastName } = person;
console.log(firstName, lastName); // Output: John Doe
```

- Destructuring allows extracting properties from objects and binding them to variables with the same name.
- It provides a more concise way to access object properties compared to dot notation.

Async/Await

Async/await is a modern approach to handling asynchronous code in JavaScript. It allows writing asynchronous code in a synchronous-like manner, making it easier to read and maintain.
Example: Async/Await

```
async function fetchData() {
 try {
 const response = await fetch('https://api.example.com/data');
 const data = await response.json();
 console.log(data);
 } catch (error) {
 console.error('Error fetching data:', error);
 }
}
fetchData();
```

- Async functions return promises implicitly, allowing them to be used with await to wait for asynchronous operations to complete.

- await suspends the execution of the async function until the promise is settled, either resolving or rejecting.

These modern JavaScript features enhance code readability, maintainability, and developer productivity, making JavaScript a more powerful and expressive language for building web applications.

Coding Exercises on Modern JavaScript Features

Modern JavaScript Features: Overview of recent ECMAScript additions and features. Here's a set of coding exercises and multiple-choice quiz questions focused on understanding and using modern JavaScript features introduced in recent ECMAScript updates. These exercises will help learners explore new syntax and functionalities that enhance code efficiency and readability.

Template Literals

Task: Use template literals to create a formatted message.
Purpose: Learn how to incorporate expressions within string literals for easier string manipulation.
JavaScript Code:

```
const user = { name: "John", age: 30 };
// Use template literals to create a formatted string
const greeting = `Hello, my name is ${user.name} and I am ${user.age} years old.`;
console.log(greeting); // Outputs: Hello, my name is John and I am 30 years old.
```

Explanation:

This exercise demonstrates how to use template literals, which allow embedded expressions and multiline strings. This feature simplifies the creation of complex strings and improves code readability.

Arrow Functions

Task: Convert a traditional function expression to an arrow function.

Purpose: Understand the concise syntax of arrow functions and their lexical scoping.

JavaScript Code:
```
const numbers = [1, 2, 3, 4, 5];
// Traditional function expression
const doubled = numbers.map(function(number) {
 return number * 2;
});
// Converted to arrow function
const doubledArrow = numbers.map(number => number * 2);
console.log(doubledArrow); // Outputs: [2, 4, 6, 8, 10]
```
Explanation:

This example shows how to simplify a function expression using an arrow function, highlighting its conciseness and the absence of its own this context, which is particularly useful in scenarios where you want to retain the scope of the outer function.

let and const

Task: Declare variables using let and const to understand their scope and immutability features.

Purpose: Differentiate between let, const, and the older var declarations.

JavaScript Code:
```
let mutable = "I can change";
```

```javascript
const immutable = "I cannot change";
console.log(mutable); // Outputs: I can change
console.log(immutable); // Outputs: I cannot change
mutable = "Changed value";
console.log(mutable); // Outputs: Changed value
// Uncommenting the line below will throw an error
// immutable = "Try changing"; // TypeError: Assignment to
constant variable.
```

Explanation:

This code introduces let and const, where let allows reassignment and has block scope, and const is also block-scoped but cannot be reassigned. This encourages using immutable data patterns in JavaScript.

Object Destructuring

Task: Extract multiple properties from an object using object destructuring.

Purpose: Simplify the extraction of multiple properties from objects.

JavaScript Code:

```javascript
const person = {
 firstName: "Jane",
 lastName: "Doe",
 age: 28,
 occupation: "Engineer"
};
// Destructure the object
const { firstName, lastName, age } = person;
console.log(`${firstName} ${lastName} is ${age} years old.`);
// Outputs: Jane Doe is 28 years old.
```

Explanation:

Object destructuring allows properties to be unpacked directly into variable declarations, making the code cleaner and easier to read, especially when working with objects containing multiple properties.

Async/Await

Task: Write an async function that fetches data from an API and logs the result using async/await.

Purpose: Demonstrate modern asynchronous JavaScript handling using async/await for more readable asynchronous code.

JavaScript Code:

```
async function fetchData() {
 try {
 const response = await
fetch('https://jsonplaceholder.typicode.com/posts/1');
 const data = await response.json();
 console.log(data);
 } catch (error) {
 console.error("Error fetching data:", error);
 }
}
fetchData();
```

Explanation:

This example uses async/await to perform asynchronous operations in a way that looks synchronous, making the code much easier to follow. Error handling is managed with try/catch, similar to synchronous code.

Multiple Choice Quiz Questions

What advantage do template literals offer over traditional string concatenation?

A) They can evaluate expressions within strings.

B) They use less memory.

C) They execute faster.

D) They can prevent variable declarations.

Correct Answer: A) They can evaluate expressions within strings.

Explanation: Template literals allow expressions to be embedded directly within strings, which simplifies the string building process and enhances readability.

Which statement about arrow functions is true?

A) They have their own this context.

B) They cannot return values.

C) They are always anonymous.

D) They can be used as constructors.

Correct Answer: C) They are always anonymous.

Explanation: Arrow functions are always anonymous and cannot have names directly assigned to them, unlike traditional function expressions or declarations.

What is the main difference between let and const?

A) let variables can be redeclared in the same scope.

B) const variables can change after initial assignment.

C) let variables can be updated, but const variables cannot.

D) const provides global scope.

Correct Answer: C) let variables can be updated, but const variables cannot.

Explanation: let allows variables to be updated within their scope. In contrast, const is used for variables that should not change after they are initially set.

How does destructuring help in handling function parameters?

A) It prevents functions from returning values.

B) It allows unpacking values directly from arrays or properties from objects.

C) It makes functions execute faster.

D) It automatically creates global variables.

Correct Answer: B) It allows unpacking values directly from arrays or properties from objects.

Explanation: Destructuring is a convenient way to extract multiple properties from objects or elements from arrays directly into variables, which can simplify how you work with function parameters (especially objects).

What does the await keyword do inside an async function?
A) Pauses the function execution until the Promise settles.
B) Stops the entire program until the Promise resolves.
C) Calls a new function to handle the next operation.
D) Automatically throws errors if the Promise rejects.
Correct Answer: A) Pauses the function execution until the Promise settles.
Explanation: Inside an async function, await pauses the execution of the function until the Promise is resolved or rejected, allowing other operations to continue running in the background.

These exercises and questions provide a robust introduction to modern JavaScript features, highlighting their practical applications and benefits in real-world programming scenarios.

JavaScript Best Practices

JavaScript Best Practices: Code organization, performance optimization, and writing maintainable code.   Here's a set of coding exercises and multiple-choice quiz questions focused on JavaScript best practices, including code organization, performance optimization, and writing maintainable code. These exercises will guide learners through effective practices that enhance code quality and maintainability.

Coding Exercises on JavaScript Best Practices

Using const for Immutable Variables

Task: Refactor code to use const for variables that should not change.
Purpose: Promote the use of immutable variables to prevent accidental reassignments and bugs.
Initial JavaScript Code:

```
let pi = 3.14159;
let daysInWeek = 7;
let maxScore = 100;
```

Refactored JavaScript Code:

```
const PI = 3.14159;
const DAYS_IN_WEEK = 7;
const MAX_SCORE = 100;
```

Explanation:
Changing let to const for variables that do not change ensures they remain immutable, reducing runtime errors due to unintentional reassignments. Additionally, naming constants in uppercase with underscores aids in distinguishing them from mutable variables.

163

Modularizing Code

Task: Break a monolithic script into smaller, function-based modules.

Purpose: Enhance code organization and reusability by creating modular components.

Initial JavaScript Code:

```javascript
function processData(data) {
 // Parse the data
 console.log("Parsing data...");
 // Process the data
 console.log("Processing data...");
 // Complete processing
 console.log("Data processing complete.");
}
processData("sample data");
```

Refactored JavaScript Code:

```javascript
function parseData(data) {
 console.log("Parsing data...");
}
function processData(parsedData) {
 console.log("Processing data...");
}
function completeProcessing() {
 console.log("Data processing complete.");
}
function runDataProcessing(data) {
 parseData(data);
 processData(data);
 completeProcessing();
}
runDataProcessing("sample data");
```

Explanation:

Breaking the processData function into smaller functions (parseData, processData, and completeProcessing) improves readability and reusability. Each function now has a single responsibility, aligning with the Single Responsibility Principle.

Optimizing Loops

Task: Optimize a loop by minimizing property accesses and method calls within the loop.
Purpose: Improve performance, especially in scenarios involving large datasets or high-frequency operations.
Initial JavaScript Code:

```
for (let i = 0; i < document.querySelectorAll('.item').length; i++) {
  console.log(document.querySelectorAll('.item')[i].textContent);
}
```

Refactored JavaScript Code:

```
const items = document.querySelectorAll('.item');
const itemsLength = items.length;
for (let i = 0; i < itemsLength; i++) {
  console.log(items[i].textContent);
}
```

Explanation:
By caching the length of the array and the DOM query result outside the loop, the browser doesn't have to recalculate the length or re-query the DOM on each iteration, leading to better performance.

Error Handling with Try-Catch

Task: Implement robust error handling in a function that might throw exceptions.
Purpose: Ensure the application remains stable and provides meaningful error information.
JavaScript Code:

```javascript
function fetchData(url) {
try {
const response = fetch(url);
const data = response.json();
console.log(data);
} catch (error) {
console.error("Failed to fetch data:", error);
}
}
fetchData("https://api.example.com/data");
```

Explanation:
Wrapping potentially error-prone code in a try-catch block helps manage exceptions gracefully, preventing the application from crashing and providing users with helpful error messages.

Using Asynchronous Patterns Properly

Task: Rewrite a callback-based function to use Promises for better error handling and flow control.

Purpose: Improve code readability and error management with Promises.

Initial JavaScript Code:

```javascript
function getData(callback) {
setTimeout(() => {
callback(null, "Data received");
}, 1000);
}
getData((err, data) => {
if (err) {
console.error(err);
} else {
console.log(data);
}
});
```

Refactored JavaScript Code:

```
function getData() {
return new Promise((resolve, reject) => {
setTimeout(() => {
resolve("Data received");
}, 1000);
});
}
getData()
.then(data => console.log(data))
.catch(error => console.error(error));
```
Explanation:
Converting the callback-based getData function into a Promise-based approach enhances error handling and simplifies chaining asynchronous operations. This also makes the function more versatile and easier to integrate with other Promise-based code.

Multiple Choice Quiz Questions

Why is it recommended to use const for variables that do not change?
A) It makes the code run faster.
B) It prevents accidental reassignment of variables.
C) It reduces the amount of memory used.
D) It is a requirement in modern JavaScript.
Answer: B) It prevents accidental reassignment of variables.
Explanation: Using const ensures that once a variable is assigned, its value cannot be changed unintentionally, promoting safer and more predictable code.

What is the benefit of modularizing code into smaller functions?
A) It decreases the memory usage of the application.
B) It increases the execution speed of the program.
C) It enhances readability and reusability of the code.
D) It automatically handles all exceptions.

Answer: C) It enhances readability and reusability of the code.

Explanation: Breaking code into smaller, function-based modules makes it easier to read, maintain, and reuse, facilitating better software design.

What is a key performance optimization technique for loops in JavaScript?
A) Placing all loop content in a single line.
B) Minimizing property accesses and method calls inside loops.
C) Using only for loops instead of while or forEach.
D) Looping in reverse order.
Answer: B) Minimizing property accesses and method calls inside loops.

Explanation: Reducing the number of property accesses and method calls within loops decreases the computational overhead in each iteration, improving performance.

What is the advantage of using try-catch for error handling?
A) It compiles the code faster.
B) It allows developers to handle errors locally where they occur.
C) It increases the security of the application.
D) It prevents users from seeing any errors.
Answer: B) It allows developers to handle errors locally where they occur.

Explanation: Try-catch blocks enable developers to manage exceptions directly within the code where errors might occur, allowing for more controlled and graceful error handling.

How do Promises improve handling asynchronous operations compared to traditional callbacks?
A) Promises allow synchronous execution of asynchronous code.
B) Promises provide better control flow and error handling.

C) Promises eliminate all potential for errors in asynchronous code.

D) Promises speed up the execution of asynchronous functions.

Answer: B) Promises provide better control flow and error handling.

Explanation: Promises simplify the management of asynchronous operations by providing a cleaner and more robust way to chain operations and handle errors, compared to the nested structure often created with callbacks (callback hell).

What is the primary use of the console.log() function in JavaScript?

A) To log errors to the console

B) To display information in the browser's console

C) To log user input

D) To debug HTML code

Answer: B) To display information in the browser's console

Explanation: console.log() is a JavaScript function that outputs a message to the web console. It is useful for testing purposes or to debug by printing out values of variables or other informational messages.

Which operator is used to check both value and type in a comparison?

A) ==

B) =

C) ===

D) !=

Answer: C) ===

Explanation: The === operator, known as the strict equality operator, compares both the value and type of two operands, ensuring that both are identical without any type coercion.

What would be the output of the following code snippet?
let x = [10, 20, 30, 40, 50]; console.log(x[2]);

A) 10

B) 20

C) 30

D) undefined

Answer: C) 30

Explanation: Arrays in JavaScript are zero-indexed. So x[2] refers to the third element in the array, which is the number 30.

Which statement creates a new object in JavaScript?

A) let obj = ();

B) let obj = {}

C) let obj = []

D) let obj = //

Answer: B) let obj = {}

Explanation: In JavaScript, curly braces {} are used to create a new object, which is a collection of key-value pairs.

What is the purpose of the Array.prototype.map() method?

A) To loop through an array's items

B) To check if any items in an array pass a test

C) To create a new array with the results of calling a function for every array element

D) To merge two or more arrays

Answer: C) To create a new array with the results of calling a function for every array element

Explanation: The map() method creates a new array populated with the results of calling a provided function on every element in the calling array.

What keyword is used to declare a variable whose value can't be reassigned?

A) let

B) var

C) const

D) static

Answer: C) const

Explanation: The const keyword is used to declare a block-scoped variable that cannot be reassigned after its initial assignment.

How do you add a comment in JavaScript?
A) <!-- This is a comment -->
B) ** This is a comment **
C) // This is a comment
D) /* This is a comment */
Answer: C) // This is a comment
Explanation: In JavaScript, comments are added using two forward slashes // for single-line comments, and /* */ for multi-line comments.

What will be logged to the console when executing console.log(typeof null);?
A) "null"
B) "undefined"
C) "object"
D) "NaN"
Answer: C) "object"
Explanation: This is a known quirk in JavaScript. The typeof a null value is "object", which is a historical bug that has remained for compatibility reasons.

Which method would you use to remove the first element from an array?
A) pop()
B) shift()
C) splice()
D) unshift()
Answer: B) shift()
Explanation: The shift() method removes the first element from an array and returns that removed element, altering the length of the array.

What does the following function declaration indicate?
function add(a, b = 2) { return a + b; }

A) The function takes two arguments and adds them.

B) The function takes one argument and adds 2 to it.

C) The function returns NaN if the second argument isn't provided.

D) The function takes two arguments, but the second has a default value of 2.

Answer: D) The function takes two arguments, but the second has a default value of 2.

Explanation: In JavaScript, you can provide default values to function parameters. In this case, if the second argument isn't provided when the function is called, b defaults to 2.

JavaScript Quick Interview Questions

Question: What is JavaScript and what are its key features?
Answer:
JavaScript is a high-level, interpreted programming language primarily used for web development. Key features include: Dynamically typed.
Supports both procedural and object-oriented programming.
Runs on the client side (web browsers).
Asynchronous programming with callbacks and Promises.

Question: Explain the difference between var, let, and const in JavaScript.
Answer:
var: Function-scoped, can be redeclared, and is hoisted.
let: Block-scoped, can be reassigned, and is hoisted.
const: Block-scoped, cannot be reassigned after declaration, and is hoisted.

Question: What is the significance of closures in JavaScript?
Answer:
Closures allow functions to retain access to variables from their outer (enclosing) scope even after the outer function has finished executing. They are crucial for creating private variables and maintaining state.

Question: Explain the event delegation in JavaScript.
Answer:
Event delegation is a technique where a single event listener is attached to a common ancestor instead of individual elements. It takes advantage of event bubbling, reducing the number of event listeners and improving performance.

Question: What is the purpose of the this keyword in JavaScript?

Answer:

this refers to the object that is currently executing the function. Its value is determined by how a function is called, and it allows access to the object's properties and methods.

Question: Describe the concept of prototypal inheritance in JavaScript.

Answer:

JavaScript uses prototypal inheritance, where objects can inherit properties and methods from other objects via a prototype chain. Each object has a prototype object, and if a property is not found in the object, JavaScript looks up the chain until it finds the property or reaches the end.

Question: What is a closure and provide an example?

Answer:

A closure is a function that has access to variables from its outer (enclosing) scope, even after the outer function has finished executing. Example:

```javascript
function outer() {
  let outerVar = 10;
  function inner() {
    console.log(outerVar);
  }
  return inner;
}
const closureFunc = outer();
closureFunc(); // Outputs: 10
```

In this example, inner forms a closure with access to outerVar.

Question: What is the difference between null and undefined in JavaScript?

Answer:

null: A deliberate assignment indicating the absence of a value.

undefined: A variable that has been declared but not assigned a value, or a non-existent property in an object.

Question: Explain the purpose of the bind method in JavaScript.
Answer:
The bind method creates a new function that, when called, has its this keyword set to a specific value. It is often used to create functions with a fixed this value.

Question: What is the difference between == and === in JavaScript?
Answer:
==: Loose equality operator, only checks for equality of values after type coercion.
===: Strict equality operator, checks for equality of values and types without type coercion.

Question: Explain the purpose of the map function in JavaScript.
Answer:
The map function is used to transform each element of an array and create a new array with the results. It does not modify the original array.
```
const numbers = [1, 2, 3];
const squaredNumbers = numbers.map(num => num * num);
// Result: [1, 4, 9]
```

Question: What is the purpose of the async and await keywords in JavaScript?
Answer:
async is used to declare an asynchronous function, and await is used to pause the execution of an async function until the promise is resolved, returning the resolved value.
```
async function fetchData() {
  const result = await fetch('https://example.com');
```

```
  const data = await result.json();
  console.log(data);
}
```

Question: Explain the concept of hoisting in JavaScript.
Answer:
Hoisting is a JavaScript behavior where variable and function declarations are moved to the top of their containing scope during compilation. However, only the declarations are hoisted, not the initializations.

Question: What is the purpose of the reduce method in JavaScript?
Answer:
The reduce method is used to accumulate values in an array and reduce it to a single value. It takes a callback function that performs the accumulation.
```
const numbers = [1, 2, 3, 4];
const sum = numbers.reduce((acc, num) => acc + num, 0);
// Result: 10
```

Question: How does event delegation work in JavaScript?
Answer:
Event delegation involves attaching a single event listener to a common ancestor, rather than attaching multiple listeners to individual elements. It leverages event bubbling, allowing the handling of events on descendant elements through a single listener.

Question: Explain the purpose of the localStorage in JavaScript.
Answer:
localStorage is a web storage object that allows developers to store key/value pairs in a web browser with no expiration time. The stored data persists even when the browser is closed and reopened.

```
// Storing data
localStorage.setItem('username', 'John');
// Retrieving data
const username = localStorage.getItem('username');
console.log(username); // Outputs: John
```

Question: How do you handle errors in JavaScript?
Answer:
Errors in JavaScript can be handled using try, catch, finally blocks.
```
try {
  // Code that might throw an error
  throw new Error('An error occurred');
} catch (error) {
  console.error(error.message);
} finally {
  // Code that always runs
}
```
Question: What is the purpose of the Promise object in JavaScript?
Answer:
Promise is an object representing the eventual completion or failure of an asynchronous operation and its resulting value. It allows better handling of asynchronous operations, especially with async/await.

Question: How does the event loop work in JavaScript?
Answer:
The event loop is a mechanism in JavaScript that allows the execution of code to be non-blocking. It consists of a call stack, callback queue, and event loop. The call stack processes synchronous code, while asynchronous code is handled through callback functions pushed to the callback queue by web APIs.

Question: Explain the concept of arrow functions in JavaScript.

Answer:

Arrow functions provide a concise syntax for writing function expressions. They do not have their own this and arguments and are not suitable for functions that require these features.

const add = (a, b) => a + b;

Question: What is the purpose of the Object.create() method in JavaScript?

Answer:

Object.create() is used to create a new object with a specified prototype object. It allows for prototypal inheritance.

```
const person = {
  greet: function() {
    console.log('Hello!');
  }
};
```

```
const john = Object.create(person);
john.greet(); // Outputs: Hello!
```

Question: Explain the concept of the event bubbling and capturing phases.

Answer:

Event propagation in the DOM occurs in two phases: capturing phase (top-down) and bubbling phase (bottom-up). Event listeners can be placed in either phase to handle events as they propagate through the DOM.

Question: What is a RESTful API, and how does it work in JavaScript?

Answer:

A RESTful API (Representational State Transfer) is an architectural style for designing networked applications. It uses standard HTTP methods (GET, POST, PUT, DELETE) for communication and is stateless. In JavaScript, the fetch API is often used to interact with RESTful APIs.

Question: What is the purpose of the setTimeout function in JavaScript?
Answer:
setTimeout is used to delay the execution of a function by a specified number of milliseconds.

```
console.log('Start');
setTimeout(() => {
  console.log('Delayed');
}, 1000);
console.log('End');
Output:
```

Start
End
Delayed

Question: How does the typeof operator work in JavaScript?
Answer:
The typeof operator returns a string indicating the type of an operand. It is often used to check the type of a variable.

```
console.log(typeof 42); // Outputs: 'number'
console.log(typeof 'Hello'); // Outputs: 'string'
console.log(typeof true); // Outputs: 'boolean'
```

Multiple Choice Quiz Questions

What will be the output of the following code?
console.log(10 + "20");
A) 30
B) "1020"
C) "30"
D) 1020
Correct Answer: B) "1020"
Explanation: In JavaScript, when a number is used with a + operator and a string, the number is converted to a string and concatenated, not added arithmetically.

Which of the following is not a primitive data type in JavaScript?
A) string
B) number
C) object
D) boolean
Correct Answer: C) object
Explanation: The object type is a complex data type, whereas string, number, and boolean are all primitive types in JavaScript.

What does the following expression evaluate to?
typeof null
A) "null"
B) "object"
C) "undefined"
D) "number"
Correct Answer: B) "object"
Explanation: This is a known quirk in JavaScript; typeof null returns "object", indicating a bug in initial JavaScript implementations.

What will be the result of the following JavaScript code?

```
let x = 5;
let y = 2;
console.log(x % y);
```

A) 2.5
B) 1
C) 5
D) 2

Correct Answer: B) 1

Explanation: The % operator returns the remainder of the division of x by y. Since 5 divided by 2 equals 2 with a remainder of 1, the result is 1.

Which operator is used to assign a value to a variable in JavaScript?

A) ==
B) =
C) ===
D) !=

Correct Answer: B) =

Explanation: The single equals sign = is the assignment operator, used to set the value of a variable.

Which of the following statements about let and const is true?

A) Variables declared with let or const are hoisted to the top of the block.
B) let allows reassignment while const does not.
C) let and const are function-scoped.
D) const variables can be declared without initialization.

Answer: B) let allows reassignment while const does not.

Explanation: Variables declared with let can be reassigned, but const is used for declaring variables meant to remain constant. Both are block-scoped, not function-scoped, and const must be initialized at the time of declaration.

What does the this keyword refer to within an arrow function?

A) The function itself

B) The global object

C) The parent scope where the arrow function was defined

D) The first argument passed to the function

Answer: C) The parent scope where the arrow function was defined

Explanation: Arrow functions do not have their own this context but inherit this from the parent scope at the time they are defined.

In JavaScript, what is a Promise?

A) A function that defers execution until a condition is met

B) An object representing the eventual completion or failure of an asynchronous operation

C) A callback function used for asynchronous operations

D) A data structure for storing multiple values

Answer: B) An object representing the eventual completion or failure of an asynchronous operation

Explanation: A Promise is an object that encapsulates the result of an asynchronous operation, allowing for more manageable asynchronous code.

Which statement correctly adds an event listener in JavaScript?

A) document.addEventListener('click', functionName());

B) document.addEventListener('click', functionName);

C) document.addEventListener.onClick(functionName);

D) document.onClick('click', functionName);

Answer: B) document.addEventListener('click', functionName);

Explanation: addEventListener is used to add an event listener, and it takes two arguments: the event type and the callback function to execute when the event is triggered.

What is NaN in JavaScript?

A) A syntax error

B) A type of exception

C) Not a Number value

D) A null reference

Answer: C) Not a Number value

Explanation: NaN stands for Not a Number, and it is a special numeric value that indicates an invalid number or a failed number conversion.

What will console.log(2 + '2'); print in JavaScript?

A) 4

B) "22"

C) "2 + 2"

D) "4"

Answer: B) "22"

Explanation: In JavaScript, using the + operator with a number and a string will result in string concatenation, thus 2 + '2' becomes "22".

What is a closure in JavaScript?

A) An error thrown by the JavaScript engine when a function finishes execution

B) The state of a function when it is paused and awaiting a callback

C) A combination of a function and the lexical environment within which it was declared

D) A method used to close a web connection

Answer: C) A combination of a function and the lexical environment within which it was declared

Explanation: A closure is a feature in JavaScript where an inner function has access to variables from an outer function's scope even after the outer function has returned.

Which HTML tag is used to include an external JavaScript file?

A) <javascript>
B) <script>
C) <js>
D) <link>

Answer: B) <script>

Explanation: The <script> tag is used to embed a JavaScript file into an HTML document with the src attribute specifying the path to the file.

What is the primary purpose of the splice() method in an array?

A) To join two arrays into one
B) To search for a specified value within the array
C) To change the contents of an array by removing or replacing existing elements and/or adding new elements
D) To reverse the order of the elements of the array

Answer: C) To change the contents of an array by removing or replacing existing elements and/or adding new elements

Explanation: The splice() method modifies the contents of an array in place and can be used to remove, replace, or add new elements to an array.

How do you declare an asynchronous function in JavaScript?

A) function async myFunc() {}
B) async function myFunc() {}
C) function myFunc() async {}
D) myFunc() = async function {}

Answer: B) async function myFunc() {}

Explanation: The async keyword is placed before the function keyword to declare an asynchronous function, which returns a Promise and allows the use of await within its body.

What is the result of trying to access a property that does not exist on an object?
A) null
B) 0
C) undefined
D) false
Answer: C) undefined
Explanation: If you attempt to access a property that has not been set on an object, JavaScript will return undefined.

How do you find the number of elements in an array named myArray?
A) myArray.count
B) myArray.size
C) myArray.length
D) count(myArray)
Answer: C) myArray.length
Explanation: The length property of an array returns the number of elements that the array contains.

What does the continue statement do in a loop?
A) Stops the loop from running any further
B) Skips the rest of the current iteration and moves on to the next one
C) Continues execution without any checks
D) Retries the current iteration
Answer: B) Skips the rest of the current iteration and moves on to the next one
Explanation: The continue statement breaks one iteration (in the loop) if a specified condition occurs, and continues with the next iteration in the loop.

What is the value of x after running this code? let x = 10; x += 5;
A) 5
B) 15

C) 10

D) undefined

Answer: B) 15

Explanation: The += operator is shorthand for x = x + 5, which adds 5 to the current value of x.

What JavaScript data type is commonly used to represent a lack of value?

A) 0

B) "" (empty string)

C) null

D) undefined

Answer: C) null

Explanation: null is an assignment value that represents a lack of any object value. It signifies 'nothing', 'empty', or 'value unknown'.

In JavaScript, what will the following code return?
Boolean(0);

A) true

B) false

C) "false"

D) 0

Answer: B) false

Explanation: In JavaScript, 0 is a falsy value. The Boolean function converts it to the boolean value false.

Which is not a valid way to declare a function in JavaScript?

A) function myFunc() { }

B) const myFunc = function() { };

C) const myFunc = () => { };

D) function = myFunc() { };

Answer: D) function = myFunc() { };

Explanation: The correct syntax for declaring a function does not assign the function to the function keyword. It either starts with the function keyword followed by the name (A), assigns a function to a constant (B), or uses an arrow function assigned to a constant (C).

What method would you use to remove duplicate values from an array in JavaScript?
A) unique()
B) distinct()
C) filter()
D) removeDuplicates()
Answer: C) filter()
Explanation: You can use the filter() method in combination with indexOf() to remove duplicates from an array by ensuring each element's index matches its first occurrence.

Which of these values is not considered a symbol in JavaScript?
A) Symbol('id')
B) Symbol.for('id')
C) Symbol.iterator
D) 'Symbol'
Answer: D) 'Symbol'
Explanation: The 'Symbol' string is not a symbol, but a primitive data type symbol can be created with Symbol('id'), retrieved from the global symbol registry with Symbol.for('id'), or be a well-known symbol like Symbol.iterator.

What is the purpose of the Array.prototype.reduce() method?
A) To execute a reducer function for array element without values
B) To decrease the size of an array by one
C) To execute a reducer function on each element of the array resulting in a single output value

D) To iterate over an array and reduce its elements to a smaller array

Answer: C) To execute a reducer function on each element of the array resulting in a single output value

Explanation: The reduce() method applies a function against an accumulator and each element in the array (from left to right) to reduce it to a single value.

Which JavaScript method is used to parse a string as JSON?

A) JSON.stringify()
B) JSON.parse()
C) JSON.toObject()
D) JSON.fromString()

Answer: B) JSON.parse()

Explanation: JSON.parse() is used to parse a string as JSON, converting it to a JavaScript object.

What will be printed to the console when executing the following code?

```
let x;
console.log(typeof x);
```

A) "null"
B) "undefined"
C) "object"
D) "string"

Answer: B) "undefined"

Explanation: The variable x is declared but not defined, so its type is "undefined".

Which statement about JavaScript arrays is true?

A) Array indexes start at 1.
B) Arrays cannot contain functions as elements.
C) Arrays are a type of object.
D) Arrays in JavaScript are immutable.

Answer: C) Arrays are a type of object.

Explanation: In JavaScript, arrays are objects that can hold a collection of items, including functions, and array indexes start at 0. They are also mutable, meaning their contents can be changed.

How do you create a function that is immediately called when defined?
A) function() {...}();
B) (function() {...})();
C) immediately function() {...};
D) function() {...} immediate;
Answer: B) (function() {...})();
Explanation: The syntax (function() {...})(); defines an Immediately Invoked Function Expression (IIFE), which runs as soon as it is defined.

What will the following JavaScript code output?
let arr = ['a', 'b', 'c', 'd', 'e'];
arr.slice(2, 4);
console.log(arr);
A) ['c', 'd']
B) ['a', 'b', 'c', 'd']
C) ['a', 'b', 'c', 'd', 'e']
D) ['c', 'd', 'e']
Answer: C) ['a', 'b', 'c', 'd', 'e']
Explanation: The slice() method does not mutate the original array but returns a new one. The original array remains unchanged.

Which of the following is not a valid way to declare a variable in JavaScript?
A) let x = 1;
B) var x = 1;
C) const x = 1;
D) int x = 1;
Answer: D) int x = 1;

Explanation: JavaScript does not have a variable type int. The valid declarations for variables are let, var, and const.

What is the output of the following code snippet?
```
let obj = {
  name: 'John',
  greet: () => console.log(`Hello, ${this.name}`)
};
obj.greet();
```
A) "Hello, John"
B) "Hello, undefined"
C) "Hello, "
D) It throws an error.
Answer: B) "Hello, undefined"
Explanation: Arrow functions do not have their own this context; they inherit it from the surrounding scope. In the global scope, this.name is undefined.

Which HTML event attribute can directly run JavaScript code when an element is clicked?
A) onclick
B) onexecute
C) onrun
D) onaction
Answer: A) onclick
Explanation: The onclick attribute is used to execute JavaScript code when an HTML element is clicked.

Which statement is true about the switch statement in JavaScript?
A) The switch statement is used to perform different actions based on multiple conditions.
B) The switch statement can only have one case for each value.
C) The switch statement is equivalent to using multiple if statements, but it is faster.

D) The switch statement is executed sequentially from the first case to the last case.

Answer: A) The switch statement is used to perform different actions based on multiple conditions.

Explanation: The switch statement evaluates an expression and executes code as per the matching case clause. It is a cleaner alternative to using many if statements but not necessarily faster.

What is the purpose of the event.preventDefault() method in JavaScript?

A) It prevents the browser from compiling JavaScript.
B) It stops the event from triggering any further.
C) It prevents the default action that belongs to the event from occurring.
D) It cancels the event if it is cancelable.

Answer: C) It prevents the default action that belongs to the event from occurring.

Explanation: The event.preventDefault() method stops the default action of the event from happening. For instance, it can prevent a link from following the URL or a form from submitting.

Which method directly modifies an array and changes its content by removing existing elements?

A) splice()
B) slice()
C) split()
D) concat()

Answer: A) splice()

Explanation: The splice() method changes the contents of an array by removing or replacing existing elements and/or adding new elements in place.

What is the result of the following expression? typeof new Date()

A) "date"
B) "object"

C) "string"
D) "time"
Answer: B) "object"
Explanation: The typeof operator returns "object" for the built-in Date object instance created by new Date().

Which of the following would set a timeout to call a function after 3 seconds?
A) setTimeout(myFunction(), 3000);
B) setTimeout(myFunction, 3);
C) setTimeout(myFunction, 3000);
D) setInterval(myFunction, 3000);
Answer: C) setTimeout(myFunction, 3000);
Explanation: setTimeout() is used to execute a function once after a specified number of milliseconds. 3000 milliseconds equals 3 seconds. Note that the function reference should be passed without invoking it (myFunction not myFunction()).

What will the following code output to the console?
console.log('10' + 20);
A) 30
B) "1020"
C) "10 20"
D) "10"+20
Answer: B) "1020"
Explanation: When you use the + operator, JavaScript converts the number into a string and performs concatenation, resulting in the string "1020".

Which object is used in JavaScript to work with regular expressions?
A) String
B) RegExp
C) Pattern
D) Match
Answer: B) RegExp
Explanation: The RegExp constructor creates a regular expression object for matching text with a pattern. It provides properties and methods for pattern matching in text.

Acknowledgements

The crafting of "JavaScript By Doing: Over 100 Coding Challenges" has been a venture steeped in commitment, fueled by a shared passion for innovation and learning. The path from conception to the final pages of this book has been brightly illuminated by the support and wisdom of countless individuals and communities.

To the vibrant web development community, I offer my profound thanks. The open-source ethos and the generous exchange of ideas within forums and collaborative platforms have provided an inexhaustible source of inspiration and practical wisdom. This book stands as a homage to the shared genius and the cooperative spirit that form the bedrock of our industry.

A special note of gratitude goes to my students, whose curiosity and insightful feedback have been instrumental in refining this work. Your eagerness to delve deeper into JavaScript's capabilities has guided the structure and substance of these pages, ensuring the material remains pertinent and responsive to your needs as learners in a dynamic technological landscape.

To you, the reader, my sincere appreciation for joining me on this journey of discovery and growth. This book is a testament to your ongoing quest for mastery in front-end development, and it is your commitment to excellence that ignites the spirit of this endeavor.

As we collectively expand the horizons of web development, I am reminded daily of the vital role each of you plays in this shared narrative. My heartfelt thanks go out to everyone who has contributed to this journey. Bound by our common zeal for technology and progress, we continue to advance, together.

About the Author

Laurence Svekis is a seasoned web developer and online educator, carrying over two decades of hands-on experience with web applications and digital learning environments. His expertise extends across JavaScript, where he has crafted and delivered educational content that simplifies complex concepts for learners at every level. Having taught over a million students across the globe, Laurence's teaching style is celebrated for its clarity and effectiveness, resonating with a diverse audience seeking to master web technologies.

In addition to his educational prowess, Laurence is an accomplished author, sharing his in-depth knowledge and practical experience in web development and programming through best-selling books. His writing is known for its actionable content, delivered in an understandable and engaging manner that reflects his passion for teaching.

As an innovative entrepreneur, Laurence remains at the forefront of web technology, focusing on creating solutions that address pressing challenges in the digital space. His entrepreneurial journey is marked by a steadfast commitment to leveraging technology to enhance learning and productivity.

Laurence's wide array of contributions has not only bolstered his reputation as an authority in web development and online education but also cemented his role as a mentor and catalyst for those venturing into the dynamic world of digital technologies. His work continues to inspire and enable countless individuals to explore and excel in the digital domain.

www.ingramcontent.com/pod-product-compliance
Lightning Source LLC
LaVergne TN
LVHW051232050326
832903LV00028B/2361